PASTA

ANNE AGER

PASTA

Exeter Books

NEW YORK

Contents

Acknowledgements
Photograph by Edmund Goldspink
Home economist   Jacki Baxter
Stylist   Emma Hartley

The author and publisher would like to thank the following companies for sponsoring photographs:
Corning Ltd (page 34); Lamberti Wines (page 38); Mushroom Growers Association (page 30); New Zealand Kiwi Fruit Information Bureau (page 74) **and** Pasta Pasta (page 46).

The author and publisher would also like to acknowledge the following companies for kindly loaning equipment for photography:
Bella Figura, Ceramic Tile Design, David Mellor, Divertimenti, Richard Dare **and** Sloane Square Tiles.

Fresh pasta and olive oil on page 46, all ham, salami, cheeses and Amaretti provided by Pasta Pasta.

Pasta for all other photography provided by the Pasta Information Centre.

Notes
All recipes serve four people, unless otherwise specified.

Flour is all-purpose, unless otherwise specified.

INTRODUCTION

The origins of pasta are steeped in myth and legend, and there is much controversy as to where it actually originated. Some people believe that the Arabs introduced pasta to the island of Sicily during the twelfth century. Others, however, hanker after the Chinese theory; it is purported that one of Marco Polo's men (named *Spaghetti*, no less!) stole the recipe for pasta from a Chinese courtesan, and brought it to Europe.

The Italians are passionate about pasta; they feel almost as strongly about pasta as they do about opera, so it is hardly surprising that they have a museum in Pontedassio dedicated to this emotive, staple food. Anyone who visits the museum, as I did several years ago, will be able to look through ancient documents, which clearly state that pasta was being eaten and enjoyed as early as 5000 BC.

Wherever the real truth lies, it is an indisputable fact that for the last two or three centuries, Italy has been the true home of pasta. Many other countries now consume pasta in quite substantial quantities, but they will never quite match the Italians at what is after all 'their own game'. Italian pasta dishes captivate the vibrant and colorful character of the country and its people: the rich deep flavors from herbs and pungent cheeses; the fruitiness of sun-ripened tomatoes and peppers; the round smooth characteristic flavor and heady aroma of virgin olive oil; and a certain robustness from wines, Marsala, plump ripe olives, and the all essential garlic!

It is hoped that this book will bring a ray of Italian sunshine into your kitchen, so that you, your family and friends can share some of the delicious pasta dishes that have their roots in Italy.

What is Pasta?

Pasta is derived from wheat – one of the world's natural foods. The endosperm, or center kernel of the wheat grain, is ground to a fine semolina and then mixed with water to a firm, smooth dough. Other ingredients such as egg and oil may also be added. Each variety of pasta has its own particular texture, dependent upon the amount of water and other ingredients within the dough. It is at this stage that the consistency of the final dough is regulated. For example, if oil is incorporated it will give a dough with a greater elasticity than one without oil.

Top quality commercially manufactured pasta is made from prime durum wheat, whereas the lesser quality pastas are made from a blend of cheaper wheats. The latter type of pasta is often soft and sticky once cooked. Durum wheat pasta, however, has a firm texture with 'a bite' to it, and the cooked pasta has a characteristic nutty flavor. How to tell? Most fresh pasta is made from durum wheat; if you are buying dried pasta, carefully check the ingredients listed on the package.

The next stage in the making of commercial pasta is the shaping; the kneaded dough is rolled out or extruded through shaped molds known as dies, giving each particular type of pasta its characteristic shape. Pasta is still quite moist and pliable at this stage, and is sold either fresh or dried in boxes or bags. The latter has been allowed to dry thoroughly in a carefully controlled temperature. Additionally, some commercial pastas are sold either frozen or canned.

For home-made pasta, see page 16.

NUTRITIONAL VALUE

Pasta is not the fattening food that it is sometimes thought to be; an average portion, about $\frac{1}{4}$ cup, amounts to about 200 calories.

The best quality pasta is a good source of protein and is considerably more nutritious than other 'starchy' foods such as potatoes, bread and rice. Wholewheat pasta is, additionally, a good source of natural fibre as it is less refined than pasta made from white flours.

The Varieties of Pasta

The pasta family is a large and varied one; it is not only the shape that differentiates one variety from another, but also the color and texture. Pasta is colored naturally; yellow pasta is plain pasta without any coloring, and the deeper the color, the more egg it contains. Green pasta gets its color and characteristic flavor from fine spinach purée. Orange pasta contains tomato purée, and brown pasta is made from wholewheat flour.

The Italians have such a wide range from which to choose that they could eat a different type on each day of the year. In most other countries the selection of pasta is more limited, but the many varieties are becoming more readily available.

Most of the pasta that is eaten outside Italy is bought in its dry, packaged form, but the availability of fresh pasta is increasing rapidly. Many supermarkets sell fresh pasta as do some speciality stores that are devoted almost exclusively to pasta in its diverse forms. Such pasta takes less time to cook, but is in every other way similar to dried pasta.

Pasta falls into three principal categories – long pasta, such as spaghetti and fettucine; shaped or short pasta such as rigatoni, twistette and farfalle, and sheet pasta, the only variety of which is lasagne. Stuffed pasta such as ravioli and cappelletti, tend to be regarded as a category on their own, but are usually grouped together with the short or shaped pastas.

Listed below are some of the most readily available varieties of pasta outside Italy. The same variety is sometimes known by more than one name, depending on the pasta manufacturer and its country of origin, so the following list only acts as a descriptive guide.

The pasta types are, incidentally, interchangeable within each category so that, for instance, bucatini can be substituted for spaghetti, if liked. Some pastas are, however, more practical to use for certain dishes than others. Generally speaking, long pastas are served with a topping sauce or are gently mixed into the sauce; shaped pastas are more robust and are mixed into their sauces while flat pastas are used for layering and baking. The smaller pasta shapes are most used in soups as they do not hold sauces well.

Category	Description	Availability
LONG PASTAS		
Bucatini	Thinner than spaghetti but not as thin as *spaghettini*	Dried
Capelli d'angelo	The thinnest of the long pastas – a very fine vermicelli, often referred to as 'angel's hair'	Dried
Fettucine	Very fine noodles, almost rod-shaped	Fresh and dried
Fusilli	Twisted spaghetti, wider than the standard spaghetti	Dried
Gemelli	Rope or plaited spaghetti	Dried
Maccheroni	The general name given to long tubular macaroni. Other shapes are sometimes also called *maccheroni*	Dried
Pappardelle	The fattest of noodles; much thicker than tagliatelle	Fresh and dried
Spaghetti	The most popular pasta. Long thin tubes of pasta available in different diameter strands	Fresh and dried
Spaghettini	The thinnest of *spaghettis*	Fresh and dried
Tagliatelle	Long ribbon noodles, wider than *fettucine*, but not as fat as *pappardelle*. Cut white noodles are often referred to as *nouilles*	Fresh and dried
Vermicelli	Very thin spaghetti, but not as thin as *Capelli d'angelo*; it usually comes curled into clusters or strands	Dried

Category	Description	Availability
SHAPED PASTAS		
Anelli	Ring-shaped pasta; the little rings are called *anellini*	Dried
Anellini rigati	Ridged, ring-shaped pasta	Dried
Cannelloni	Although this usually comes under the category of 'shaped pasta', it is actually made from flat or sheet pasta, formed into large hollow pasta tubes	Fresh and dried
Conchiglie	This is the term generally used for all shell-shaped pastas. Sizes vary somewhat, and the tiny shells are known as *conchigliette*	Fresh and dried
Ditali	A form of cut macaroni, shorter than *elbow maccheroni*, and sometimes called *thimble macaroni*	Dried
Elbow maccheroni	Curved short lengths of macaroni; even the Italians refer to it as elbow maccheroni	Dried
Farfalle	Butterfly or bow-shaped pasta; the smallest ones are called *farfallette*; the slightly larger size *farfalline*, and the largest butterfly pasta *farfalloni*	Dried
Lumache	Medium-sized snail-shaped pasta	Dried
Lumachine	Small pasta snails	Dried

Chart continues over.

Category	Description	Availability
Orzo	Small pasta shapes resembling plump long-grain rice	Dried
Penne	Diagonally cut tubes of pasta, cut from tubular macaroni	Dried
Rigatoni	Large ridge-shaped pasta tubes	Fresh and dried
Stelline	Small star-shaped pasta	Dried
Twistette	Stubby spirals of pasta	Fresh and dried

SHEET PASTAS

Lasagne	Completely flat sheet pasta	Fresh and dried
Lasagne riccie	Rippled sheets of *lasagne*	Dried

FILLED PASTAS

Agnolotti	Half-moon *raviolo*	Dried
Cappelletti	Pasta shaped into 'little hats', and stuffed with a savory filling	Fresh and dried
Ravioli	Squares of pasta sandwiched with a savory filling	Fresh and dried
Tortelline	Small twists of pasta stuffed with a savory filling	Fresh and dried

Although most of the pasta types mentioned above are fairly widely available outside Italy. there are within Italy itself distinctive preferences for certain varieties according to region. Generally, the South tends to favor ready-made packaged spaghetti and noodles, whereas the Northern Italians prefer the shaped pastas, especially the shaped and filled varieties such as ravioli.

Storage of Pasta

Fresh/Dried	Cooked/Uncooked	Storage Life	Freezing
COMMERCIAL PASTAS			
Fresh pre-packed	Uncooked	Use by 'best by' date	Pack in easily usable quantities in polythene bags, excluding air. Twist tie and freeze for 6 months. Cook from frozen.
	Cooked	Overnight only	Undercook slightly, drain, cool and pack in polythene bags. Store for 1 month only. Put into boiling water, bring back to boil and cook for a few minutes until *al dente*
Freshly made	Uncooked	Wrap in plastic wrap and store in a refrigerator for 48 hours	As commercial fresh
	Cooked	Overnight only	As commercial fresh
Dried	Uncooked	6 months – unopened 2 weeks – opened	— —
	Cooked	Overnight only	As fresh
Commercially frozen	Uncooked	—	Store for 1 month only. Cook from frozen, following manufacturer's instructions
HOME-MADE	Cooked	Overnight only	As commercial fresh
Fresh	Uncooked	Overnight only	As commercial fresh
	Cooked	Overnight only	As commercial fresh

THE FLAVORS OF PASTA COOKING

The style of cooking varies very much from one part of Italy to another, and the dishes not only reflect locally available produce, but also the prosperity of the particular region. The most marked difference is that between the North and South of the country; the North of Italy is generally more wealthy, and the people eat a lot of meat, dairy produce and egg-enriched pasta. The Italians in the South, however, exist on a more economical diet, yet it is none the less colorful – locally produced olives and olive oil, fish which is abundant in the coastal regions, home-made goat cheeses and manufactured pasta.

Italian pasta dishes echo these regional characteristics, but they also encapsulate the overall color, aroma and flavor of a wide variety of Italian produce. It is these ingredients which lend that very authentic flavor to pasta – glossy red and green peppers, and bright purple egg plants; juicy citrus fruits (oranges, lemons and limes); a wide variety of fresh herbs, such as basil, oregano, thyme and parsley; spices such as coriander, saffron and ginger; and the two most important ingredients in any Italian kitchen – olive oil and garlic.

Olive oil is used extensively in pasta dishes, both for tossing the cooked pasta and for preparing the sauces. Use a good quality olive oil wherever possible, as it makes a great deal of difference to the flavor.

Garlic is the other main-stay of pasta cooking, but for some people it is an acquired taste. If you only like a subtle garlic flavor, then use a bruised clove which can be removed easily; if, however, you prefer a stronger more traditional flavor, crush or finely chop the garlic before adding it to the pasta sauce (this will vary according to the particular recipe).

Fresh herbs make an enormous difference to the final flavor of a pasta dish, and it is worth all the effort involved in obtaining them. Several fresh herbs can be bought from most good supermarkets. If you find these difficult to obtain locally, then you can use one-third the quantity of the equivalent dried herb. Basil is the most widely used herb in Italian cooking, not just for pasta, but it is also one of the most difficult to grow; it does not like cold climates, and the specially cultivated and imported varieties tend, therefore, to be fairly expensive. Even so, it is worth remembering that for most dishes you only need about three leaves which means that any you do not use can be frozen. With spices, it is advisable to buy the whole varieties, and crush or grind them as required; the dried, ready prepared ones tend to lose their characteristic flavor very quickly.

Cheese and pasta are particularly complimentary to one another, and the appropriate variety of cheese is normally chosen very carefully. The very hard Italian cheeses, such as Pecorino and Parmesan, are finely grated and usually used to sprinkle over cooked pasta dishes; they are sometimes also used in the preparation. The softer, easy-melting cheeses, such as Bel Paese, Fontina and Mozzarella are frequently added to made-up pasta dishes prior to cooking, such as Lasagne al Forno (see page 34).

Tomatoes are another important Italian ingredient. The big mis-shapen plum tomatoes have a much fuller sweeter flavor than the average-sized regular tomato. If you find these difficult to buy, you can always use good quality canned ones. Many tomato-based sauces are served with pasta, and the canned ones drained in water rather than in fresh tomato juice, are excellent for such sauces – drain well before using.

Most cooked pasta dishes comprise a sauce, either as a serving accompaniment or as part of the made-up dish. Tomato sauces have already been mentioned, but a classic Italian pasta sauce is Pesto; it can be bought either ready-made from most good supermarkets, or you can make your own at home (see page 65).

Wine and Marsala are essential ingredients in many pasta sauces; they contribute a fullness of flavor and a native robustness.

Freshly ground black pepper may sound a very basic ingredient, but I have intentionally extracted it from the other pasta flavorings. Several pasta dishes are very simple in make-up, yet it is the careful and distinctive seasoning that completes the finished dish. Salt is important, but for really good pasta, black pepper is essential.

The popularity of pasta has created both an extension and a development in its uses. The USA, for instance, is particularly keen on pasta salads – both simply prepared side salads with dressings and vegetables – and more substantial salads made with fish or meat which serve as main-course dishes.

Pasta as Mama Makes It!

Fresh pasta has already been mentioned, (see page 8) and nothing quite beats the home-made article. Most Italian mamas have developed a strong right arm over the years, from kneading endless batches of pasta dough, and it is a time-consuming and demanding job. The satisfaction of kneading pasta by hand is very similar to the feeling achieved when making home-made bread. For those who do not feel up to the rigors of pulling and punching pasta dough, there are several short-cuts. The basic dough can be made in a food mixer fitted with a dough hook, or in a food processor fitted with a paddle blade; this eliminates the pulling and punching by hand. Alternatively, it is possible to buy small machines that will actually make the pasta dough as well as shaping it. They do, however, tend to be quite expensive, but are worth purchasing if you plan on making a lot of pasta. If it is the shaping of the actual pasta that worries you, then there are many gadgets to come to your aid, ie a hand operated pasta machine, which will cut noodles (eg fettucine and tagliatelle) and sheet pasta of different widths at the turn of a handle, a noodle 'wheel' which can be run along the full length of the rolled out pasta dough, and a ravioli form.

Home-made pasta is not difficult to make, but you do need to be patient and have plenty of time. If you are a gifted bread and pastry maker, then you will find it extremely easy.

Making pasta at home can be a messy business and you need to allow yourself plenty of room; you can use a very large chopping board or a marble slab, or alternatively, you can roll out the prepared dough on a clean kitchen work surface. If you are rolling the dough by hand (and not by machine), then an extra long rolling-pin is particularly useful.

Pasta is best made from a good strong flour (one that has plenty of gluten content) so that the dough will roll and stretch readily. It is not essential to add eggs to a home-made pasta dough, but it does make it more easy to handle and shape, especially for first time makers. Although the quantity of oil used is relatively small, it is important that it should be olive oil; other oils will not give such a good flavor.

A selection of equipment for making different types of pasta

Pasta all'Uova
BASIC PASTA DOUGH – ENRICHED WITH EGG

Makes 1lb

This dough can be used for making all types of pasta.

2 cups flour
1 teaspoon salt
4 eggs, beaten
1 tablespoon olive oil

Sift the flour and salt into a mound on a clean work surface. Make a well in the center, then add the eggs and olive oil. Gradually draw in the flour from the edges and work together to a smooth dough. Knead the dough vigorously on a well floured surface until it is firm, very smooth and elastic. (This can be done in an electric mixer or food processor as mentioned on page 14). You should be able to stretch the kneaded dough without its surface cracking and crazing. This will take about 20 minutes, depending on how practised you are at kneading, and whether you do it by hand or by machine. Cover the prepared pasta dough with a damp clean towel and leave it to relax for 30 minutes.

Divide the dough into two or three portions, depending on how much space you have. Roll each portion of dough out very thinly on a floured surface, lifting it from time to time to ensure that it is fully stretched and has not stuck. The secret of really good home-made pasta is to get it rolled out extremely thinly; you should be able to lift the rolled dough up to the light and see dark objects through it!

Sheets of lasagne are usually cut by hand to suit the size of the dish to be used. For fettucine or tagliatelle, hang the rolled sheets of dough on a clean floured towel, over the back of a chair. Leave to relax for 10 minutes, then roll the sheets of dough up loosely, as for a jelly roll. Using a very sharp knife, cut the roll of pasta dough at regular intervals, to give even-sized strips – ¼ inch for fettucine, and ½ inch for tagliatelle. (If you have a pasta shaping machine, you can regulate the thickness of the dough by adjusting the numbered dial close to the turning handle; the rolled dough can then be fed back into the machine and cut into noodles, either the size of fettucine or tagliatelle.)

The shaped pasta can either be cooked immediately or it can be hung over the back of a chair on a clean towel and left to dry for 1–2 hours.

Variations

Wholewheat Pasta
Use 1 cup wholewheat flour and 3 cups flour. Make as for Basic Pasta Dough.

Pasta Verde
Add 3–4 tablespoons sieved cooked spinach to the flour, eggs and olive oil when working to a smooth dough.

Ravioli
Roll out the prepared pasta dough as thinly as possible into four even-sized rectangles. Place small spoonfuls of filling 1½ inches apart in straight lines on two sheets of the dough. Run a dampened pastry brush in straight lines between the filling, then lay the two remaining sheets of pasta over the top of each filled sheet. Press down firmly between each mound of filling to seal the two layers of dough. Cut the ravioli into 2 inch squares by running a pastry wheel or sharp knife in straight lines along the pressed areas. Separate the squares of ravioli and use as required.

If you have a simple hand ravioli form (this looks rather like an ice-cube tray), roll out the prepared pasta dough as thinly as possible. Lightly grease the form and lay a sheet of rolled dough over it; press it carefully into each indentation. Brush the raised areas of dough, between the divisions, with water or beaten egg. Put a small spoonful of filling into each indentation, then lay another sheet of rolled dough over the top. Roll across the top of the form with a short rolling-pin to sandwich the filling between the two layers of dough and to divide it into small squares of ravioli. Use as required.

Alternatively, ravioli can be prepared using a special rolling-pin with notched squares on its surface. The ravioli squares are formed by rolling the pin over the pasta.

Another way of preparing ravioli is by using a special attachment to a standard pasta shaping machine, as for other pasta types.

For the filling, use either a very thick Bolognese Sauce (see page 29) or a mixture of half cooked spinach, well drained, and half ricotta or sieved cottage cheese.

Other Home-made Shaped Pastas
Roll out the prepared dough as thinly as possible and prepare your own shapes, eg bows, twists, etc.

Cooking, Serving and Eating Pasta

Pasta is a very simple food to cook, but it does not always receive the careful attention which it deserves. It is very easy to ruin if not cooked correctly, and few things are less appetizing then soggy, overcooked pasta. Whether you are cooking fresh or dried pasta, the same general rules apply; only the length of cooking time varies (see below).

1) Bring a large solid-based pan of water to the boil, allowing approximately 2 quarts water per 1½ cups pasta.

2) Add 1 tablespoon olive oil and 1 teaspoon salt to the pan as the water comes to the boil. The oil prevents the pasta from sticking and the salt will bring out the essential flavor of the pasta.

3) Lower the pasta into the pan carefully, keeping the water on the boil. For long pasta, such as spaghetti, 'curl' it gradually around the inside of the pan; add short pasta in spoonfuls to the boiling water. Slide large pasta such as lasagne into the water individually to prevent the sheets sticking together; count 10 between each addition.

4) Stir the pasta *once* only to separate the individual strands or shapes. Do not stir any more otherwise starch is released unnecessarily and this will affect the final texture of the pasta.

5) Cook at a rolling boil until the pasta is just *al dente* (ie firm to the bite).

Suggested cooking times for principal pasta types

Pasta type	Fresh	Dried
Spaghetti	3 minutes	8–9 minutes
Fettucine	2–3 minutes	5–10 minutes (according to make)
Tagliatelle	2–3 minutes	5–10 minutes (according to make)
Pasta shapes (eg farfalle, conchiglie, etc)	2–3 minutes	6–8 minutes
Filled pasta (eg ravioli etc)	3–4 minutes	6–8 minutes
Vermicelli	—	1–2 minutes
Lasagne	— (pre-cooking)	6 minutes (pre-cooking)

Note The cooking times of other pasta types can be determined by comparing their size with some of those listed above.

6) To test, take a little of the pasta from the pan and bite it; it should be firm to the tooth yet tender (ie *al dente*).

7) Drain the cooked pasta thoroughly in a large sieve or colander. Do not rinse pasta.

SERVING AND EATING PASTA

The Italian approach to serving and eating pasta is very different to that in many other countries. In Italy, pasta is often served as part of a complete meal, in fact as a separate pasta dish. This is not to say that pasta is never served as the sole dish of a meal with a simple salad or two.

It is a common mistake to serve pasta in portions that are too large; this is why it has inherited the reputation for being over-filling and fattening. Pasta should be served to enhance the appetite and not to discourage or dampen it, and you should be able to leave the table afterwards without feeling over-full.

As a general guide, allow approximately $\frac{1}{4}$ cup pasta (uncooked) per person for a starter or dessert and $\frac{1}{3}$ cup pasta (uncooked) for a main course. Heavily sauced, very rich pasta dishes are best reserved for serving as a main meal with a salad, whereas simple pasta dishes are perfect to start a meal. Pasta salads can be served as a course in their own right. Allow about $\frac{1}{3}$ cup pasta (uncooked) per person for a simple salad and $\frac{1}{4}$ cup pasta (uncooked) for a more elaborate salad with added protein or one to be served as a starter. Alternatively, a selection of different pasta salads can be served with salamis and other Italian cold meats as a mixed hors d'oeuvre. Soups do not require more than about 3 tablespoons pasta (uncooked) per person.

Serve cooked pasta piping hot and serve made-up pasta dishes, such as lasagne, on pre-warmed plates. Accompanying salads are always served in separate bowls or on small side plates so that the temperature of the pasta does not wilt the salad. Make sure that the ingredients used in a side salad complement those used in the pasta dish, ie, if the flavor of the pasta and its sauce are fairly strong, keep the salad very simple, with a reasonably bland dressing.

There is an art in eating long pasta, such as spaghetti and tagliatelle, which is why many people would prefer not to eat it in public; they would prefer to make a fool of themselves in the privacy of their own homes. The Italians, however, are nowhere near as self-conscious; they have few inhibitions, and many of them look positively barbaric when eating pasta, using their forks like shovels and their noses touching their food! It is an art that is so simple to master, that there need never be any embarrassment. Children nearly always manage to make a mess when eating pasta, however good their table manners, and it is a good idea to tie a large napkin around their necks before they start eating.

The implements needed for eating pasta are minimal; some people like to use a spoon and a fork, but a fork is all that is really necessary for long pasta, pasta shapes and even made-up pasta dishes. Stick the prongs of your fork into the long pasta, and twist it round and round until you have a manageable mouthful. Lift the fork up from your plate, allowing any loose strands of pasta to drop off, and pop the forkful quickly into your mouth.

FOR PASTA PROFESSIONALS

I came back from my last visit to Italy with the most wonderful gadget; a special pasta fork! It looked just like any other fork, apart from the fact that there was a small turning handle set into the end of the wooden fork handle. You push the prongs of the fork into a portion of long pasta, and, holding the fork steady, you rotate the turning handle; it automatically winds the pasta around the prongs of the fork. Perhaps a gimmick, but very successful!

PASTA SOUPS

Italian soups are often served as a complete meal, and this is why so many contain pasta – usually a small shaped pasta. Thin soups generally have their pasta cooked in them while thick soups use pasta which has been cooked separately so that the pasta is not lost in the natural thickness of the soup.

Pasta soups do not necessarily need an accompaniment, but most people find them rather 'naked' eaten on their own. Crusty Italian-style bread is perfect, or you can, of course, serve grissini and a bowl of tangy grated cheese, such as Parmesan or Pecorino.

Broth is a very important ingredient in all soup making, and home-made broth is always preferable. There are recipes in this chapter for Brodo di Pollo (chicken broth) and for Brodo di Manzo (beef broth), both of which are simple to prepare and make a vast difference to the finished dish.

BRODO DI POLLO
BASIC CHICKEN BROTH

Makes 1½ quarts broth

1 large chicken
1 veal shank (8 oz approx)
3 quarts water
2 large carrots, roughly chopped
1 large onion, roughly chopped
2 stalks celery, chopped
2 bay leaves
a bunch of parsley stalks
a few sprigs rosemary
1 teaspoon crushed peppercorns

Put the chicken into a large pan with the veal shank and the water, and bring to the boil slowly. Remove any surface scum with a slotted spoon. Add the remaining ingredients and bring back to the boil, then cover, reduce the heat and simmer gently for 2½–3 hours.

Strain the prepared broth through a piece of clean muslin or cheesecloth. Store, covered, in a refrigerator for up to 4 days.

Variation
To serve the broth as a clear soup, clarify it first. Put the strained broth into a clean pan and add two crushed egg shells and two stiffly beaten egg whites. Bring to the boil, stirring all the time, then strain again through clean muslin or cheesecloth.

Cook pasta in the cleared soup.

19

BRODO DI MANZO
BASIC BEEF BROTH

Makes 1½ quarts broth

2 lb beef bones
3 medium carrots
2 medium onions
3 quarts water
1 lb shin of beef, roughly chopped
2 stalks celery, chopped
a small bunch of parsley stalks
2 bay leaves
1 teaspoon crushed peppercorns
½ teaspoon crushed mustard seed

Put the beef bones, carrots and onions into a roasting pan, and bake in a hot oven, 400°F for 30 minutes until really well browned.

Put the browned bones, carrots and onions into a pan and add the water. Bring to the boil slowly, then remove any surface scum with a slotted spoon. Add the remaining ingredients and bring back to the boil. Cover, reduce the heat and simmer gently for 3 hours.

Strain the prepared broth through a piece of clean muslin or cheesecloth. Store, covered, in a refrigerator for up to 4 days.

Variation
Clarify as for Brodo di Pollo (page 19).

ZUPPA DI BROCCOLI ALLA ROMANA
BROCCOLI SOUP

2 tablespoons olive oil
1 large onion, finely chopped
2 oz Parma ham, cubed (see **Note**)
1 large clove of garlic, crushed
1 quart Brodo di Pollo (chicken broth, page 19)
8 oz broccoli
salt, freshly ground black pepper
¼ cup stelline (small pasta stars)
½ cup grated Parmesan cheese

Heat the oil in a large pan. Add the onion and Parma ham and cook gently for 4–5 minutes, then add the garlic and chicken broth. Bring to the boil, then reduce the heat and simmer for 10 minutes.

Meanwhile, blanch the broccoli by simmering the florets in boiling salted water for 5 minutes. Drain thoroughly and add to the broth with the stelline. Season to taste with salt and pepper, then simmer the soup for 2 minutes until the pasta is tender. Serve in warmed soup bowls and sprinkle each portion with grated Parmesan cheese.

Note Small cubes of Parma ham can be bought from many good delicatessens and supermarkets, at a much cheaper price than the sliced variety.

PASTA E FAGIOLI
PASTA AND BEAN SOUP

¾ cup dried pea beans
1 large onion, sliced
2 large carrots, sliced
2 stalks celery, sliced
1 large clove of garlic, finely chopped
1 small ham bone
2 quarts Brodo di Pollo (chicken broth, page 19)
½ cup elbow maccheroni
2 tablespoons olive oil
½ cup grated Parmesan cheese
2 tablespoons chopped parsley
salt, freshly ground black pepper

Soak the beans for 8 hours or overnight in cold water. Drain
them, then put into a large pan with the onion, carrots, celery,
garlic, ham bone and chicken broth. Bring to the boil, then
reduce the heat and simmer gently until the beans are tender.
Drain off about half the cooked beans from the soup and pass
them through a sieve. Remove the ham bone and trim off any
small pieces of meat. Return the sieved beans and chopped ham
to the soup and bring back to the boil. Add the maccheroni and
simmer steadily for 2–3 minutes until the pasta is tender. Stir in
the oil, grated cheese, parsley and seasoning to taste. Serve
piping hot in warmed soup bowls.

RAVIOLI IN BRODO
CHICKEN AND RAVIOLI SOUP

1 quart Brodo di Pollo (chicken broth, page 19)
4 tablespoons chopped parsley
6 oz fresh ravioli (any filling is suitable)
salt, freshly ground black pepper

GARNISH

4 tablespoons olive oil
4 tablespoons stale coarse breadcrumbs
1 small clove of garlic, crushed

Put the chicken broth into a large pan and bring to the boil.
Add the parsley and ravioli, and bring back to the boil. Reduce
the heat and simmer steadily until the ravioli is just tender.
  Meanwhile, prepare the garnish. Heat the oil in a pan and fry
the crumbs and garlic until crisp and golden.
  Season the soup to taste, and serve in warmed soup bowls.
Sprinkle with the fried breadcrumbs.

Zuppa di Pomodoro con Polpettine
TOMATO SOUP WITH MEATBALLS AND PASTA

1 slice of white bread, $\frac{1}{2}$ inch thick, broken into
large pieces
4 tablespoons milk
$\frac{1}{4}$ cup butter
1 large onion, finely chopped
8 oz lean veal **or** pork, finely ground
1 teaspoon chopped fresh sage
salt, freshly ground black pepper
a generous pinch of ground nutmeg
2 egg yolks
2 medium carrots, grated
$1\frac{1}{2}$ lb plum tomatoes, skinned, seeded and chopped
1 clove of garlic, crushed
1 quart Brodo di Manzo (beef broth, page 20)
2 cups dry white wine
$\frac{1}{3}$ cup vermicelli

Mix the bread with the milk, then leave to stand for 10 minutes. Squeeze the bread to remove excess moisture. Melt 25g/1 oz of the butter in a pan and gently fry half the onion until soft. Mix with the squeezed bread, the ground meat, sage, seasoning to taste, nutmeg and egg yolks, and mould into small balls about the size of an olive. Chill for 30 minutes.

Meanwhile, melt the remaining butter and fry the remaining onion for 3–4 minutes. Add the carrots, tomatoes, garlic, beef stock and wine, and bring to the boil, then reduce the heat and simmer for 45 minutes.

Press the soup through a sieve into a clean pan. Bring the soup back to the boil and add the prepared meatballs. Reduce the heat and simmer gently for 12 minutes, then add the vermicelli and simmer for a further 2 minutes. Adjust seasoning to taste. Serve the soup in warmed deep soup bowls.

Minestra di Verdura
VEGETABLE AND HAM MINESTRONE

2 tablespoons olive oil
2 oz pork **or** ham fat, chopped
1 large onion, finely chopped
2 large carrots, chopped
3 stalks celery, chopped
4 oz spinach, shredded
4 oz green cabbage, shredded
salt, freshly ground black pepper
3 tablespoons finely chopped parsley
1 tablespoon chopped fresh marjoram
6 oz piece bacon **or** gammon, skin removed
1 small pig's foot
$1\frac{1}{2}$ quarts Brodo di Pollo (chicken broth, page 19)
$\frac{1}{3}$ cup nouilles (broken noodles)

Heat the oil in a large pan, add the chopped fat and cook until the fat runs free. Add the onion, carrots and celery, and fry gently for 5 minutes, then add the remaining ingredients apart from the noodles. Bring to the boil, then reduce the heat and simmer for about 45 minutes until the bacon and meat on the foot are tender.

Remove the piece of bacon and the foot from the soup. Chop the bacon and remove the meat from the foot bone in small pieces. Add the chopped meats to the soup. Bring the soup back to the boil and add the broken noodles. Stir steadily for 2–3 minutes until the pasta is tender. Serve the soup in large warmed soup bowls.

Zuppa di Pomodoro con Polpettine

Minestra di Crostacei
LOBSTER AND TOMATO MINESTRONE

1 medium lobster, cooked
5 cups water
salt, freshly ground black pepper
¼ cup butter
1 small onion, finely chopped
1 lb plum tomatoes, skinned, seeded and chopped
1 clove of garlic, crushed
¾ cup dry white wine
2 tablespoons finely chopped parsley
½ cup stelline (small pasta stars)

Split the lobster lengthways. Pull out the intestinal tract and clear out the head cavity. Remove the gills. Remove the meat carefully from the shell, and dice it.

Put the shell into a pan with the water and salt and pepper to taste. Bring to the boil, then reduce the heat and simmer for 20 minutes. Strain and reserve the lobster broth.

Melt the butter in a large pan and gently fry the onion for 4 minutes. Add the chopped tomatoes and garlic, and fry gently for a further 2 minutes. Add the strained lobster broth, the white wine and parsley, and simmer for 10 minutes. Add the diced lobster meat and the stelline, and simmer for 2 minutes until the pasta is just tender. Serve the soup piping hot.

Note A store may well prepare the lobster, if necessary.

Zuppa di Gamberi
SHRIMP AND BASIL SOUP

2 tablespoons olive oil
2 tablespoons butter
2 medium carrots, chopped
3 stalks celery, cut into strips
1 tablespoon chopped fresh basil
2 tablespoons chopped parsley
1 medium onion, finely chopped
salt, freshly ground black pepper
8 oz shelled shrimp
1 quart Brodo di Pollo (chicken, broth page 19)
¾ cup Marsala
⅓ cup farfalle (pasta bows)
4 tablespoons heavy cream

GARNISH (optional)
unpeeled shrimp

Heat the oil and butter in a large pan. Add the carrots, celery, basil, parsley and onion, and fry gently for 5 minutes. Season to taste, then add the shrimp and chicken broth. Bring to the boil, then reduce the heat and simmer for 20 minutes. Add the Marsala and bring back to the boil. Add the farfalle and simmer gently for 5–6 minutes until the pasta is tender. Stir in the cream, adjust seasoning to taste, and heat through. Serve the hot soup in warmed soup bowls, garnishing each portion with one or two unpeeled shrimp, if liked.

ZUPPA DI CASTAGNE CON LUMACHINE
CHESTNUT SOUP WITH SMALL PASTA SNAILS

8 oz chestnuts
$\frac{1}{4}$ cup butter
1 large onion, finely chopped
2 medium carrots, finely chopped
1 celery stalk, finely chopped
salt, freshly ground black pepper
$4\frac{1}{2}$ cups Brodo di Manzo (beef broth, page 20)
$1\frac{1}{2}$ cups dry white wine
3 tablespoons medium sherry
$\frac{1}{3}$ cup lumachine (small pasta snails)

Score the shell of each chestnut. Put them on to a cookie sheet and bake in a warm oven, 325°F for 15 minutes. Peel off the shells and skins from the chestnuts while they are still warm.

Melt the butter in a large pan and cook the onion, carrots and celery until lightly golden. Add the chestnuts, salt and pepper to taste, the broth and the wine. Bring to the boil, then reduce the heat and simmer until the chestnuts are quite tender. Blend the soup in a liquidizer or food processor, or sieve it until smooth. Return to a clean pan, add the sherry and heat through gently.

Meanwhile, cook the lumachine in a pan of boiling salted water until just tender. Drain thoroughly and add to the soup. Serve in warmed soup bowls.

ZUPPA DI CAPELLI D'ANGELO
VERMICELLI AND ZUCCHINI SOUP

2 tablespoons butter
2 tablespoons olive oil
1 small onion, finely chopped
8 oz zucchini, cut into $\frac{1}{4}$ inch thick slices
salt, freshly ground black pepper
1 quart Brodo di Pollo (chicken broth, page 19)
$\frac{3}{4}$ cup dry white wine
2 eggs
1 tablespoon chopped parsley
1 tablespoon chopped fresh basil
$\frac{1}{4}$ cup grated Parmesan cheese
$\frac{1}{3}$ cup capelli d'angelo (very fine vermicelli)

Heat the butter and oil in a large pan. Add the onion and fry gently for 2–3 minutes. Add the zucchini and fry for a further 2–3 minutes. Season to taste. Add the broth and wine and bring to the boil, then reduce the heat and simmer for 15 minutes.

Beat the eggs with the parsley, basil and Parmesan cheese. Beat a little of the hot soup liquor into the egg mixture, and then return the egg mixture to the remaining soup. Bring the soup back just to the boil, then add the vermicelli. Reduce the heat and simmer for 2 minutes. Serve the soup in warmed soup bowls.

Zuppa alla Paesana
Peasant-Style Lentil Soup

1½ cups dried lentils
salt, freshly ground black pepper
1 tablespoon olive oil
2 tablespoons butter
4 stalks celery, sliced
1 small head of fennel, shredded
1 large clove of garlic, crushed
2 tablespoons chopped parsley
1 lb ripe plum tomatoes, skinned,
seeded and roughly chopped
1 quart Brodo di Manzo (beef broth, page 20)
¼ cup wholewheat pasta rings
2 tablespoons grated Parmesan cheese

GARNISH

4 feathery sprigs fennel

Soak the lentils in cold water for 6 hours or overnight, then drain them and put into a pan. Add enough fresh cold water just to cover, and 1 teaspoon salt. Cover, bring to the boil and simmer for about 50 minutes – 1 hour until the lentils are just tender.

Meanwhile, heat the oil and butter in a large pan. Add the celery and fennel and fry gently for 5 minutes. Add the garlic, parsley, tomatoes and beef stock. Bring to the boil, then reduce the heat and simmer for 15 minutes. Drain the cooked lentils and add to the soup.

Cook the pasta rings in a pan of boiling salted water until just tender. Drain thoroughly and add to the soup. Season to taste with salt and pepper, and heat through. Serve the soup in warmed soup bowls. Sprinkle each portion with a little grated Parmesan cheese and garnish with a sprig of fennel.

Zuppa di Ceci
Chick-Pea and Pasta Soup

1½ cups dried chick-peas
salt, freshly ground black pepper
2 sprigs fresh rosemary
1 bay leaf
2 tablespoons olive oil
6 anchovy fillets, drained and chopped
1 large clove of garlic, crushed
6 ripe plum tomatoes, skinned, seeded and
roughly chopped
1 quart Brodo di Pollo (chicken broth, page 19)
⅓ cup lumachine (small pasta snails)

Soak the chick-peas in plenty of cold water for 6 hours or overnight. Drain them, put into a pan, and add sufficient fresh cold water just to cover them. Add 1 teaspoon salt, the rosemary and bay leaf. Bring to the boil, then reduce the heat and simmer for about 45 minutes until the chick-peas are tender. Remove the rosemary and bay leaf. Blend the chick-peas and their cooking liquor in a liquidizer or food processor, or sieve until smooth.

Heat the oil in a large pan, add the anchovy fillets and garlic and fry gently for 1 minute. Add the tomatoes and chicken broth and simmer for 10 minutes, then stir in the puréed chick-peas and simmer for 5 minutes.

Meanwhile, cook the lumachine in a pan of boiling salted water until just tender. Drain thoroughly and add to the hot soup. (If necessary, thin the soup down with a little extra hot broth). Season to taste with salt and pepper, and serve in warmed soup bowls.

Pasta e Fagioli (page 21), Zuppa alla Paesana **and** *Zuppa di Gamberi (page 24)*

ZUPPA VERDE CON SPAGHETTINI
WATERCRESS AND SPAGHETTINI SOUP

2 bunches watercress, trimmed and chopped
2 onions, sliced
1 quart Brodo di Pollo (chicken broth, page 19)
salt, freshly ground black pepper
⅓ cup spaghettini, broken into 2 inch lengths

GARNISH

2 hard-cooked eggs, finely chopped

Put the watercress into a pan with the onions, broth and salt and pepper to taste. Bring to the boil, then reduce the heat and simmer for 15 minutes. Add the spaghettini and simmer for a further 4 minutes until the pasta is tender. Serve in warmed soup bowls, topped with chopped hard-cooked egg.

ZUPPA DI VERDURE CON FARFALLETTE
LEEK AND PASTA SOUP

Serves 4–6

2 tablespoons butter
1 onion, finely chopped
2¼ lb leeks, sliced
1 large potato, peeled and sliced
1 quart Brodo di Pollo
(chicken broth, page 19)
salt, freshly ground black pepper
¾ cup farfallette (small pasta bows)

Melt the butter in a large pan and gently fry the onion for 5 minutes. Add the leeks and potato and cook for 5 minutes. Add the broth and bring to the boil. Season to taste, then cover, reduce the heat and simmer until the leeks are cooked. Blend the soup in a liquidizer or food processor, or sieve until smooth, then return to the pan. Add the farfallette and simmer for 2–3 minutes until the pasta is tender. Serve the soup in warmed soup bowls.

PASTA AS A MAIN COURSE

If you mention pasta to many people, they will think immediately of Spaghetti Bolognese. This is not necessarily an insult to pasta, merely a simple fact that they are unaware as to the permutations that pasta has to offer as a main meal. It is such a versatile food that it can be served as an appetizer as in Italy, in which case the recipes which follow will serve six rather than four people. The richer, more elaborate, pasta recipes should, however, be kept as main courses. Fish, meat, poultry and eggs all blend particularly well with pasta, offering a great repertoire of main meal dishes, some extremely simple and others a little more complicated.

A simple way of serving pasta is to toss the cooked, drained pasta very quickly in melted butter or a good quality olive oil, adding salt and freshly ground black pepper and grated nutmeg or chopped fresh herbs, if liked. Stir briefly over gentle heat, and spoon into warmed bowls. Serve immediately with grated Parmesan cheese.

The pasta and sauces are best prepared in a heavy-based pan so that there is no danger of the pasta or other ingredients sticking to the pan.

Vegetables can be served as an accompaniment to a pasta main dish, but a really good tossed salad is more complimentary. Vary the salad ingredients according to the main course recipe. Crisp lettuce always makes a good base. For a fish pasta, add finely shredded raw fennel; for game or poultry, try using a few nuts and perhaps also some peeled orange sections; for meat-based pasta dishes, add a little thinly sliced raw onion, slivers of radish and chopped pepper, and for pasta dishes using egg, add ripe olives, chopped anchovy fillets or capers to the salad. Fresh herbs, when available, lift a salad into the super class.

SPAGHETTI ALLA BOLOGNESE
SPAGHETTI WITH MEAT SAUCE

$\frac{1}{3}$ cup butter
2 tablespoons olive oil
4 oz smoked **or** cured Italian ham, chopped
1 medium onion, finely chopped
2 stalks celery, finely chopped
8 oz ground beef
6 oz chicken livers, chopped
4 oz mushrooms, chopped
2 tablespoons tomato paste
$\frac{3}{4}$ cup Brodo di Manzo (beef broth, page 20)
$\frac{3}{4}$ cup red wine
2 tablespoons Marsala
1 large clove of garlic, crushed
salt, freshly ground black pepper
2 tablespoons heavy cream
$1\frac{1}{2}$ cups spaghetti

GARNISH

2 tablespoons chopped parsley

Heat $\frac{1}{4}$ cup butter and 1 tablespoon olive oil in a pan. Add the chopped ham and onion and fry gently for 3 minutes. Add the chopped celery, ground beef and chicken livers and stir over heat until evenly browned. Add the remaining ingredients, apart from the leftover butter and oil and the spaghetti. Bring to the boil, then reduce the heat and simmer the sauce for 30 minutes.

Meanwhile, cook the spaghetti in a large pan of steadily boiling water until *al dente* with the remaining oil and 1 teaspoon salt. Drain thoroughly, then melt the remaining butter and toss the spaghetti in it. Pile on to a hot serving plate and spoon the hot Bolognese sauce over the top. Sprinkle with chopped parsley, and serve with a bowl of grated Parmesan or Pecorino cheese.

Note The Bolognese sauce is also known as *Ragu*.

SPAGHETTI ALLA CARBONARA
SPAGHETTI WITH BACON AND EGG SAUCE

Serves 4–6

1½ cups spaghetti
4 tablespoons olive oil
salt, freshly ground black pepper
1 medium onion, finely chopped
6 slices bacon, rinds removed and chopped
6 tablespoons dry white wine
4 eggs
⅓ cup grated Pecorino cheese
1 large clove of garlic, crushed
1 tablespoon chopped fresh basil

Cook the spaghetti in a large pan of steadily boiling water until *al dente* with 1 tablespoon olive oil and 1 teaspoon salt.

Meanwhile, heat the remaining olive oil in a pan, add the onion and fry gently for 4 minutes. Add the chopped bacon and fry for a minute or two. Add the white wine, and boil briskly until nearly all the liquid has evaporated. Beat the eggs with the Pecorino cheese, garlic, basil and salt and pepper to taste.

Drain the cooked spaghetti thoroughly and quickly stir in the beaten egg mixture and the bacon so that the heat from the pasta lightly cooks the egg. Serve immediately.

CANNELLONI CON SALAME
SALAMI STUFFED CANNELLONI

6 oz fresh lasagne **or** dry packaged lasagne
2 tablespoons olive oil
salt, freshly ground black pepper
1 large onion, chopped
4 oz mushrooms, sliced
8 oz salami, diced
1 lb plum tomatoes, skinned, seeded and chopped
1 tablespoon cornstarch
3 cups Salsa Beschiamella
(savory white sauce, page 64)
1 cup grated Pecorino cheese

GARNISH

sprigs parsley

If using dried lasagne, pre-cook it in a pan of steadily boiling water for about 6 minutes with 1 tablespoon olive oil and 1 teaspoon salt. Use fresh lasagne as it is.

Meanwhile, heat the remaining oil in a pan and cook the onion until soft. Add the mushrooms and soften them, then add the salami and tomatoes. Mix together well. Blend the cornstarch with a little water to form a smooth paste, then add to the salami mixture. Simmer for 2 minutes until the mixture has thickened. Season well.

Drain the dried lasagne thoroughly, cut the sheets in half (fresh or dried) and place the salami mixture in the center. Roll them up and place either in four greased individual ovenproof dishes (three to a dish) or in one large ovenproof dish.

Mix the sauce with half the grated cheese, then pour it over the cannelloni and sprinkle with the remaining cheese. Cook in a fairly hot oven, 375°F, until golden-brown. Garnish with sprigs of parsley and serve immediately.

Serve with a crisp salad.

Cannelloni con Salame

SPAGHETTINI TETRAZZINI
BAKED SPAGHETTI WITH BACON AND CHICKEN

¾ cup spaghettini
1 tablespoon olive oil
salt, freshly ground black pepper
6 oz bacon, rinds removed and chopped
2 red peppers, seeded and chopped
8 oz cooked chicken, chopped
3 tablespoons butter
6 tablespoons flour
¾ cup milk
2 cups Brodo di Pollo (chicken broth, page 19)
⅓ cup grated Bel Paese cheese
¼ teaspoon grated nutmeg
2 tablespoons sherry
1 egg yolk
2 tablespoons flaked almonds

Cook the spaghettini in a large pan of steadily boiling water until *al dente* with the oil and 1 teaspoon salt.

Meanwhile, fry the bacon and peppers gently in a large pan until the bacon is crisp but not brown. Add the chicken and cook for a further 5 minutes. Drain the pasta thoroughly and gently stir into the mixture, then remove from the heat.

Melt the butter in a clean pan, add the flour, then slowly add the milk and broth. Bring to the boil, stirring constantly, and leave the sauce to thicken. Add the cheese, then season to taste with salt and pepper and add the nutmeg and sherry. Off the heat, stir in the egg yolk.

Place the chicken mixture in an ovenproof dish, coat with the sauce and sprinkle with the flaked almonds. Cook in a fairly hot oven, 375°F, for about 25 minutes until bubbling and golden. Serve immediately.

MACCHERONI CON SALAME E VERDURE
MACARONI WITH SALAMI AND VEGETABLES

4 tablespoons olive oil
1 medium onion, finely chopped
1 large clove of garlic, crushed
1 lb plum tomatoes,
skinned, seeded and chopped
1 sweet red pepper, seeded and cut into strips
8 oz zucchini, thinly sliced
6 oz Italian salami, cubed
salt, freshly ground black pepper
1½ cups elbow maccheroni
3 tablespoons butter, melted

Heat 3 tablespoons olive oil in a pan. Add the onion and fry gently for 3 minutes. Add the garlic and chopped tomatoes and bring to the boil. Reduce the heat and simmer steadily until the tomatoes are really soft and pulpy. Add the pepper, zucchini, salami and salt and pepper to taste, and simmer until the vegetables are just tender.

Meanwhile, cook the maccheroni in a large pan of steadily boiling water until *al dente* with the remaining oil and 1 teaspoon salt. Drain thoroughly and toss in the melted butter. Gently stir in the prepared hot vegetable and salami sauce. Serve immediately.

TAGLIATELLE VERDE AMATRICIANA
TAGLIATELLE WITH BACON AND PARMESAN SAUCE

¼ cup butter
1 medium onion, thinly sliced
¾ cup dry white wine
8 oz lean bacon, rinds removed and chopped
1 tablespoon chopped basil
1 tablespoon chopped parsley
1 lb plum tomatoes, skinned, seeded and chopped
salt, freshly ground black pepper
1½ cups tagliatelle verde
1 tablespoon olive oil
⅓ cup grated Parmesan cheese

Melt the butter in a pan and cook the onion until golden. Add the wine, bacon, herbs, tomatoes and salt and pepper to taste. Simmer gently for 15 minutes, stirring occasionally.

Meanwhile, cook the tagliatelle in a large pan of steadily boiling water until *al dente* with the oil and 1 teaspoon salt. Drain thoroughly and pile on to a hot serving dish. Spoon the hot sauce over the top to coat thoroughly. Sprinkle generously with Parmesan cheese, toss and serve immediately.

CARCIOFFI CON PASTA
PASTA STUFFED ARTICHOKES

Serves 6

6 globe artichokes
1 lemon
salt, freshly ground black pepper
2 tablespoons butter
1 medium onion, finely chopped
1½ cups Salsa Besciamella
(savory white sauce, page 64)
3 eggs, separated
⅓ cup grated Parmesan cheese
4 oz lean Italian ham, finely chopped
2 tablespoons tagliatelle verde, broken into pieces

Cut a 1 inch slice from the top of each artichoke. Trim off the tip of each leaf with kitchen scissors. Halve the lemon and rub all the cut surfaces of the artichokes with half the lemon. Bring a large pan of water to the boil. Add 1 teaspoon salt and the juice from the remaining half lemon to the pan. Add the prepared globe artichokes, cover the pan and simmer steadily for about 25 minutes until the artichokes are tender. Pull on one of the lower leaves and if it comes away readily the artichoke is ready. Drain the cooked artichokes, cut surfaces downwards, on absorbent kitchen paper.

Melt the butter in a pan and gently fry the chopped onion for 3 minutes. Stir in the sauce, egg yolks, two-thirds of the Parmesan cheese, salt and pepper to taste, and the chopped ham.

Remove the center leaves from each artichoke (these can be used in soup), and the center 'hairy choke'. Stand the hollowed artichoke upright in a greased baking pan.

Cook the tagliatelle in boiling salted water for about 3–4 minutes until tender, then drain thoroughly. Meanwhile, whisk the egg whites until stiff but not dry.

Fold the egg whites and cooked tagliatelle into the sauce mixture lightly but thoroughly. Spoon carefully into the center of each hollowed artichoke, and sprinkle with the remaining grated Parmesan cheese. Cook in a fairly hot oven, 375°F, for about 40–50 minutes until the centres are risen and golden. Serve immediately before the centers of the artichokes have a chance to collapse.

Lasagne di Carne Misto
Turkey and Italian Ham Lasagne

Serves 4–6

¼ cup butter
1 medium onion, finely chopped
¼ cup flour
1½ cups Brodo di Pollo (chicken broth, page 19)
¾ cup milk
a pinch of grated nutmeg
salt, freshly ground black pepper
4 oz Italian ham, finely chopped
8 oz cooked turkey, finely chopped
6 oz fresh lasagne verde **or**
dry packaged lasagne (see **Note**)
4 oz mushrooms, sliced
juice of 1 lemon
1 cup sour cream
1 egg
¾ cup grated Pecorino cheese

Melt half the butter in a pan and cook the onion until soft. Stir in the flour and cook for 1 minute. Gradually add the broth and milk, and bring to the boil, stirring constantly, until the sauce has thickened. Add the nutmeg, salt and pepper to taste, the ham and the chopped turkey.

Spread one-third of the sauce over the base of a greased rectangular au gratin pan; arrange one-third of the lasagne on top, and repeat until the sauce and lasagne are used. Finish with a layer of lasagne.

Melt the remaining butter in a clean pan and gently cook the mushrooms with the lemon juice. Arrange them on top of the lasagne. Beat the sour cream with the egg and spoon this evenly over the mushrooms. Sprinkle with the grated cheese. Cook in a fairly hot oven, 375°F, for 30–35 minutes until bubbling and golden. Serve immediately.

Note If using dry packaged lasagne, use only the variety which requires no previous cooking.

Lasagne al Forno
Baked Meat Lasagne

Serves 4–6

3 tablespoons olive oil
2 oz Italian ham, chopped
1 medium onion, finely chopped
1 lb ground sirloin
1 large clove of garlic, crushed
3 tablespoons tomato paste
1 pint Brodo di Pollo (chicken broth, page 19)
salt, freshly ground black pepper
6 oz fresh lasagne **or** dry packaged lasagne (see **Note**)
8 oz Bel Paese **or** Fontina cheese,
rinds removed and thinly sliced
1½ cups Salsa Besciamella
(savory white sauce, page 64)
3 tablespoons grated Parmesan cheese

Heat the oil in a large pan. Add the chopped ham and cook for 1–2 minutes to extract the fat. Add the chopped onion and fry gently for 4 minutes. Add the ground beef and cook until evenly browned. Add the garlic, tomato paste, broth and salt and pepper to taste. Cover, bring to the boil, then reduce the heat and simmer gently for 45 minutes.

Spread one-third of the meat sauce over the base of a greased rectangular au gratin pan; arrange one-third of the lasagne on top, and follow with one-third of the Bel Paese or Fontina cheese. Repeat with two more layers of meat sauce, lasagne and sliced cheese. Spoon the prepared Sauce evenly over the top, then sprinkle with the grated Parmesan cheese. Cook in a fairly hot oven, 375°F, for about 45 minutes until bubbling and golden. Serve immediately.

Note If using dry packaged lasagne, use only the variety which requires no previous cooking.

Lasagne di Carne Misto

FUSILLI ALLA CARUSO
SPAGHETTI WITH LIVER AND MUSHROOM SAUCE

1½ cups fusilli (twisted spaghetti)
4 tablespoons olive oil
salt, freshly ground black pepper
1 medium onion, finely chopped
1 clove of garlic, crushed
6 oz calf's liver, chopped
4 oz mushrooms, sliced
12 oz plum tomatoes,
skinned and sieved
1 teaspoon chopped parsley

Cook the fusilli in a large pan of steadily boiling water until *al dente* with 1 tablespoon oil and 1 teaspoon salt.

Meanwhile, heat the remaining oil in a pan and cook the onion until soft, then add the crushed garlic. Add the liver and cook gently for 2 minutes, then add the mushrooms, tomatoes and parsley. Simmer for 4–5 minutes and season to taste.

Drain the cooked pasta thoroughly and gently stir in the prepared hot sauce. Serve immediately.

TAGLIATELLE CON SALSA DI PROSCIUTTO
TAGLIATELLE WITH HAM AND MUSHROOM SAUCE

1½ cups tagliatelle verde
1 tablespoon olive oil
salt, freshly ground black pepper
2 tablespoons butter
8 oz Italian ham, chopped
4 oz mushrooms, sliced
1½ cups Salsa Beschiamella
(savory white sauce, page 64)
4 tablespoons heavy cream

Cook the tagliatelle in a large pan of steadily boiling water until *al dente* with the oil and 1 teaspoon salt.

Meanwhile, melt the butter in a pan and cook the chopped ham for 2 minutes. Remove from the pan and cook the mushrooms in the remaining fat. Transfer the ham and mushrooms to a clean pan and mix together with the sauce and salt and pepper to taste. Stir in the cream and heat through.

Drain the pasta thoroughly and arrange around the outside of a dish. Pour the sauce into the center and serve immediately.

Pasta e Pollo
PASTA AND CHICKEN SCALLOPS

1½ cups ditali (thimble macaroni)
4 tablespoons olive oil
salt, freshly ground black pepper
1 large onion, finely chopped
4 slices bacon, rinds removed and chopped
8 oz mushrooms, chopped **or** sliced
1 cup heavy cream
8 oz cooked chicken, chopped
4 tablespoons fresh breadcrumbs
⅓ cup grated Bel Paese **or** Fontina cheese

GARNISH

sprigs parsley

Cook the pasta in a large pan of steadily boiling water until *al dente* with 1 tablespoon olive oil and 1 teaspoon salt.

Meanwhile, heat the remaining oil in a pan and cook the onion for 2 minutes. Add the bacon and mushrooms and cook for a further 3–4 minutes. Drain the pasta thoroughly and stir into the mixture with the cream and chopped chicken. Season to taste with salt and pepper, then spoon into four greased scallop shells or one large au gratin pan. Sprinkle with the breadcrumbs and the grated cheese and brown under a medium broiler. Garnish with parsley sprigs.

Maccheroni al Forno
MACARONI AND SHRIMP LAYER BAKE

1½ cups maccheroni
1 tablespoon olive oil
salt, freshly ground black pepper
¼ cup butter
6 oz mushrooms, finely sliced
6 oz shelled shrimp
3 cups Salsa Beschiamella
(savory white sauce, page 64)
½ cup grated Parmesan cheese

GARNISH

unpeeled shrimp

Cook the maccheroni in a large pan of steadily boiling water until *al dente* with the oil and 1 teaspoon salt.

Meanwhile, melt the butter in a pan and cook the mushrooms until soft. Add the shrimp off heat, then mix them with the sauce, and season to taste with salt and pepper.

Drain the pasta thoroughly, then fill a buttered ovenproof dish with alternate layers of pasta and shrimp and mushroom sauce, starting with pasta and finishing with the sauce. Sprinkle with the Parmesan cheese and cook in a fairly hot oven, 375°F, for 20–25 minutes until bubbling. Garnish with whole shrimp and serve immediately.

LASAGNE ALLA PESCE
FISH LASAGNE

Serves 4–6

12 oz cooked white fish, flaked
7 oz canned tuna drained and coarsely flaked
3 cups Sugo di Pomodoro e Panna
(tomato and cream sauce, page 72)
2 tablespoons chopped parsley
4 anchovy fillets, drained and chopped
salt, freshly ground black pepper
4 tomatoes, skinned, seeded and chopped
⅓ cup plump ripe olives, pitted and chopped
2 teaspoons capers
6 oz fresh lasagne **or** dry packaged lasagne (see **Note**)
8 oz Mozzarella cheese, thinly sliced
2 tablespoons fine breadcrumbs
2 tablespoons olive oil

Mix the white fish with the tuna, tomato and cream sauce, parsley, anchovy fillets, salt and pepper to taste, chopped tomatoes, olives and capers. Spread one-third of the mixture over the base of a greased rectangular au gratin pan; arrange one-third of the lasagne on top, and follow with one-third of the Mozzarella cheese. Repeat with two more layers of fish and sauce mixture, lasagne and sliced cheese. Sprinkle the top with the breadcrumbs and olive oil. Cook in a fairly hot oven, 375°F, for about 45 minutes until bubbling and golden. Serve immediately.

Note If using dry packaged lasagne, use only the variety which requires no previous cooking.

Variation
Use flaked canned or fresh cooked salmon in place of the canned tuna.

PAPPARDELLE ALLA PUTTANESCA
NOODLES WITH TOMATO AND ANCHOVY SAUCE

2 tablespoons olive oil
3 cloves garlic, chopped
1½ lb beef tomatoes skinned, seeded and chopped
1 tablespoon fresh oregano, chopped
6 anchovy fillets, drained and chopped
12 ripe olives
1 tablespoon capers
salt, freshly ground black pepper
1½ cups pappardelle (wide ribbon noodles)

GARNISH

chopped parsley

Heat 1 tablespoon olive oil in a pan and cook the garlic until golden. Add the chopped tomatoes, the oregano, anchovies, olives and capers. Season to taste with salt and pepper, and simmer for about 15 minutes, stirring frequently.

Meanwhile, cook the pappardelle in a large pan of steadily boiling water until *al dente* with the remaining oil and 1 teaspoon salt. Drain thoroughly, then pile on to a hot serving dish and spoon the sauce over the top. Toss carefully, then sprinkle with chopped parsley and freshly ground pepper. Serve immediately.

Pappardelle alla Puttanesca

MACCHERONI CON GAMBERI
MACARONI WITH SHRIMP

Serves 4–6

¾ cup elbow maccheroni
1 tablespoon olive oil
salt, freshly ground black pepper
3 oz shelled shrimp
2 eggs, beaten
3 tablespoons sour cream
5 tablespoons breadcrumbs
2 tablespoons butter

Cook the pasta in a large pan of steadily boiling water until *al dente* with the oil and 1 teaspoon salt. Drain thoroughly, then mix together with the shrimp, eggs and sour cream. Season to taste with salt and pepper. Transfer to a greased au gratin pan, top with the breadcrumbs and dot with small knobs of butter. Cook in a fairly hot oven, 375°F, for 25 minutes until bubbling. Serve immediately.

TAGLIATELLE AL TONNO
TAGLIATELLE WITH TUNA AND MUSHROOM SAUCE

1½ cups tagliatelle verde and plain tagliatelle
1 tablespoon olive oil
salt, freshly ground black pepper
7 oz canned tuna
1 medium onion, chopped
4 oz mushrooms, sliced
¾ cup heavy cream

Cook the tagliatelle in a large pan of steadily boiling water until *al dente* with the oil and 1 teaspoon salt.

Meanwhile, drain the oil from the tuna into a large pan, and cook the chopped onion until soft. Add the sliced mushrooms and cook until soft, then season to taste with salt and pepper.

Drain the pasta thoroughly and add to the pan. Pour in the cream and mix together over low heat. Adjust seasoning to taste and serve immediately.

Pasta alla Pescatore
FISHERMAN'S PASTA

1 cup elbow maccheroni
1 tablespoon olive oil
salt, freshly ground black pepper
2 tablespoons butter
½ cup light cream
grated rind of ½ lemon
2 tablespoons chopped parsley
7 oz canned tuna, drained and flaked
4 oz shelled shrimp

GARNISH

unshelled shrimp
sprigs parsley

Cook the pasta in a large pan of steadily boiling water until *al dente* with the oil and 1 teaspoon salt.

Meanwhile, melt the butter in a pan and stir in the cream, lemon rind, chopped parsley, flaked tuna and shelled shrimp.

Drain the pasta thoroughly and add to the pan. Season to taste with salt and pepper, and heat through gently. Garnish with a few unshelled shrimp and parsley sprigs. Serve immediately.

Fettucine alla Gorgonzola
FETTUCINE WITH GORGONZOLA SAUCE

1½ cups fettucine
2 tablespoons olive oil
salt, freshly ground black pepper
4 slices bacon, rinds removed and chopped
1 large clove of garlic, crushed
1½ cups light cream
6 oz Gorgonzola, finely crumbled
1 tablespoon chopped fresh sage

Cook the fettucine in a large pan of steadily boiling water until *al dente* with 1 tablespoon olive oil and 1 teaspoon salt.

Meanwhile, heat the remaining oil in a pan and fry the chopped bacon for 3–4 minutes. Add the garlic, cream, crumbled Gorgonzola, sage and salt and pepper to taste, and heat through.

Drain the cooked fettucine thoroughly and gently stir in the prepared hot sauce. Serve immediately.

PASTA PASTICCIATA
PASTA PIE

Serves 6

¾ cup vermicelli
salt, freshly ground black pepper
3 tablespoons olive oil
5 eggs, beaten
freshly grated nutmeg
2 tablespoons finely chopped parsley
1 medium onion, thinly sliced
12 oz cold cooked spinach, chopped
4 oz cream cheese, softened
¾ cup light cream
1 tablespoon chopped fresh basil
2 tablespoons grated Pecorino cheese

Cook the vermicelli in boiling salted water for 2 minutes, then drain thoroughly. Mix with salt and pepper to taste, 1 tablespoon of the olive oil, two beaten eggs, a little freshly grated nutmeg and the chopped parsley. Press the noodle mixture over the base and up the sides of a greased 9 inch flan dish. Cover the rim of the pasta with foil and cook in a fairly hot oven, 375°F, for 10 minutes until set.

Meanwhile, heat the remaining oil in a pan and gently fry the sliced onion for 5 minutes. Mix with the spinach and salt, pepper and nutmeg to taste. Beat the cream cheese with the cream and remaining eggs until smooth.

Mix together the spinach and cream cheese mixtures, and add the chopped basil. Spread the filling evenly into the pasta shell and sprinkle with the Pecorino cheese. Bake for a further 25–30 minutes until the filling is set. Serve warm, cut into wedges.

SPAGHETTI CON FORMAGGIO E NOCE
SPAGHETTI WITH RICOTTA AND ALMONDS

½ cup ground almonds
4 oz ricotta
a pinch of ground cinnamon
a pinch of grated nutmeg
¾ cup light cream
4 tablespoons olive oil
¼ cup grated Parmesan cheese
salt, freshly ground black pepper
1½ cups spaghetti
¼ cup butter, melted
1 tablespoon chopped parsley

GARNISH

flaked toasted almonds

Mix together the ground almonds with the ricotta, cinnamon, nutmeg, cream and 3 tablespoons of the oil to make a thick paste. Add the Parmesan cheese and salt, and mix well.

Cook the spaghetti in a large pan of steadily boiling water until *al dente* with the remaining oil and 1 teaspoon salt. Drain thoroughly, reserving ¼ pint of the water. Toss the spaghetti in the butter and chopped parsley and pile on to a warm serving dish.

Mix together the reserved water and the ricotta sauce and pour this over the spaghetti. Garnish with a few flaked toasted almonds and serve immediately.

Pasta Pasticciata

CONCHIGLIE AL FORMAGGIO
CHEESE AND PASTA SCALLOPS

Serves 4–6

1½ cups conchiglie (pasta shells)
1 tablespoon olive oil
salt, freshly ground black pepper
6 slices bacon, rinds removed
3 hard-cooked eggs, chopped
3 cups Salsa Beschiamella
(savory white sauce, page 64)
1½ cups grated Bel Paese cheese

Cook the pasta in a large pan of steadily boiling water until *al dente* with the oil and 1 teaspoon salt.

Meanwhile, grill the bacon until crisp, then cut into small pieces. Drain the pasta thoroughly, then mix with the bacon and chopped egg, reserving some of the bacon for the garnish.

Season the sauce to taste and add half the grated cheese. Arrange the pasta mixture in 4–6 large greased scallop shells, then top with the sauce and sprinkle with the remaining cheese and the reserved bacon pieces. Place under the broiler for 5 minutes until browned. Serve immediately.

RAVIOLI CON BESCIAMELLA
RAVIOLI WITH WHITE SAUCE AND CHEESE

12 oz fresh ravioli (see **Note**)
1 tablespoon olive oil
salt, freshly ground black pepper
3 tablespoons butter, melted
1½ cups Salsa Besciamella
(savory white sauce, page 64)
2 tablespoons light cream
4 oz Mozzarella cheese, thinly sliced
2 tablespoons grated Parmesan cheese

Cook the ravioli in a large pan of steadily boiling water until *al dente* with the olive oil and 1 teaspoon salt. Drain thoroughly and toss in the melted butter. Spoon the ravioli into a lightly greased shallow ovenproof dish. Mix the sauce with the cream and season to taste with salt and pepper. Spoon the sauce evenly over the ravioli. Lay the slices of Mozzarella on top and sprinkle with the grated Parmesan cheese. Cook in a fairly hot oven, 375°F, for 15 minutes until the sauce is lightly golden and bubbling. Serve immediately.

Note Any filling is suitable for the ravioli.

FETTUCINE ALL'ALFREDO
FETTUCINE IN CREAM AND BUTTER SAUCE

1½ cups fettucine
1 tablespoon olive oil
salt, freshly ground black pepper
¼ cup butter
1 clove of garlic, finely chopped
½ cup grated Parmesan cheese
freshly grated nutmeg
1 tablespoon chopped fresh basil
1 cup heavy cream

Cook the fettucine in a large pan of steadily boiling water until *al dente* with the oil and 1 teaspoon salt.

Meanwhile, melt the butter in a pan and cook the garlic for 1 minute.

Drain the cooked fettucine thoroughly and gently stir into the pan with the Parmesan cheese, salt, pepper and nutmeg to taste, the basil and the cream. Stir over gentle heat for 1 minute and serve immediately.

CAPPELLETTI CON LA PANNA
STUFFED PASTA HATS WITH BUTTER AND CREAM

1½ cups cappelletti (stuffed pasta hats)
1 tablespoon olive oil
salt, freshly ground black pepper
¾ cup heavy cream
¼ cup butter, melted
½ cup grated Parmesan cheese
1 tablespoon chopped fresh coriander

Cook the cappelletti in a large pan of steadily boiling water until *al dente* with the oil and 1 teaspoon salt. Drain thoroughly.

Put the cream, melted butter, Parmesan cheese, coriander and salt and pepper to taste into a clean pan. Add the cooked pasta and stir over gentle heat for 1 minute. Serve immediately.

FETTUCINE CON SALSA DI NOCE
FETTUCINE WITH WALNUT SAUCE

1½ cups fettucine
1 tablespoon olive oil
salt, freshly ground black pepper
¼ cup butter
3 oz walnuts, finely chopped
1 large clove of garlic, crushed
3 tablespoons grated Parmesan cheese
4 tablespoons Brodo di Pollo (chicken broth, page 19)
2 tablespoons sour cream

Cook the fettucine in a large pan of steadily boiling water until *al dente* with the oil and 1 teaspoon salt.

Meanwhile, melt half the butter in a pan. Add the walnuts and garlic, and fry for 1 minute. Stir in the grated cheese and the chicken broth over heat.

Drain the cooked fettucine thoroughly, melt the remaining butter and toss the pasta in it, together with the sour cream. Season to taste with salt and pepper. Serve the pasta in individual bowls, topped with the hot walnut sauce.

Serve with a green salad.

FETTUCINE CON FAGIOLI
FETTUCINE WITH BEANS

1¼ cups fettucine
5 tablespoons olive oil
salt, freshly ground black pepper
3 cloves garlic, finely chopped
a generous pinch of chilli powder
15 oz canned red kidney beans, drained
2 teaspoons Pesto (page 65)
6 oz Mozzarella cheese, diced

Cook the fettucine in a large pan of steadily boiling water until *al dente* with 1 tablespoon olive oil and 1 teaspoon salt.

Meanwhile, heat the remaining olive oil in a pan and fry the garlic gently without allowing it to color. Stir in the chilli powder, red kidney beans, Pesto and salt and pepper to taste.

Drain the cooked fettucine thoroughly and gently stir in the hot oil and bean mixture. Immediately stir in the diced Mozzarella cheese so that it starts to soften and melt before serving.

Fettucine con Fagioli

GEMELLI CON FETA
SPAGHETTI WITH FETA CHEESE AND BROWN BUTTER

1½ cups gemelli (plaited spaghetti)
1 tablespoon olive oil
salt, freshly ground black pepper
⅓ cup butter
2 oz pitted ripe olives, chopped
6 oz Feta cheese, coarsely crumbled
1 tablespoon chopped fresh sage

Cook the gemelli in a large pan of steadily boiling water until *al dente* with the oil and 1 teaspoon salt.

Meanwhile, melt the butter in a large pan and heat until it turns nutty brown in color. Stir in the chopped olives, the Feta cheese, sage and salt and pepper to taste.

Drain the cooked pasta thoroughly and toss in the hot nutty butter until evenly coated. Serve immediately.

LUMACHE AL MASCHERPONE E NOCE
PASTA SNAILS WITH CREAM CHEESE AND WALNUTS

1½ cups lumache (pasta snails)
1 tablespoon olive **or** walnut oil
salt, freshly ground black pepper
2 tablespoons butter
6 oz cream cheese
3 oz walnuts, coarsely chopped

Cook the lumache in a large pan of steadily boiling water until *al dente* with the oil and 1 teaspoon salt.

Meanwhile, melt the butter in a pan. Add the cream cheese and stir until melted and smooth. Season to taste with salt and pepper, and add the chopped walnuts.

Drain the cooked lumache thoroughly and toss in the cream cheese and walnut mixture. Serve immediately.

Pasta con Pesto
PASTA WITH PESTO

2 medium potatoes, peeled and thinly sliced
salt, freshly ground black pepper
1½ cups fettucine
1 tablespoon olive oil
2 tablespoons butter, melted
2 tablespoons Pesto (page 65)
1 tablespoon poppy seeds

Cook the sliced potatoes in a pan of boiling salted water until just tender (they should still hold their shape).

Meanwhile, cook the fettucine in a large pan of steadily boiling water until *al dente* with the oil and 1 teaspoon salt.

Drain the fettucine and potatoes thoroughly and toss lightly together with the melted butter, Pesto and poppy seeds. Serve immediately.

Tortellini alla Panna
STUFFED PASTA TWISTS IN HERBED CREAM

12 oz fresh tortellini (small stuffed pasta twists)
1 tablespoon olive oil
salt, freshly ground black pepper
½ cup light cream
1 tablespoon chopped fresh basil
1 tablespoon chopped fresh tarragon
1 clove of garlic, crushed
a generous pinch of freshly grated nutmeg

Cook the tortellini in a large pan of steadily boiling water until *al dente* with the olive oil and 1 teaspoon salt.

Meanwhile, heat the cream gently in a large shallow pan and add the chopped fresh herbs, the garlic, nutmeg and salt and pepper to taste.

Drain the cooked pasta thoroughly and stir it into the hot herbed cream. Heat through for 1–2 minutes.

Ravioli alla Piemontese
RAVIOLI WITH MUSHROOM AND TOMATO SAUCE

⅓ cup butter
1 medium onion, thinly sliced
8 oz mushrooms, finely chopped
1 lb plum tomatoes, skinned, seeded and chopped
2¼ cups Brodo di Manzo (beef broth, page 20)
12 oz fresh ravioli
1 tablespoon olive oil
salt, freshly ground black pepper

Melt half the butter in a pan and cook the onion, mushrooms and tomatoes until tender. Add the broth and simmer for 20 minutes.

Meanwhile, cook the ravioli in a large pan of steadily boiling water until *al dente* with the oil and 1 teaspoon salt. Drain thoroughly. Melt the remaining butter and toss the ravioli in it. Off heat, add the sauce, and season to taste with salt and pepper. Mix thoroughly and serve immediately.

Fusilli alla Contadina
SPAGHETTI WITH BROCCOLI AND BREADCRUMB SAUCE

1½ cups fusilli (twisted spaghetti)
1 lb broccoli
9 tablespoons olive oil
salt, freshly ground black pepper
2 cloves garlic, chopped
5 anchovy fillets, drained and chopped
1 red chilli pepper
1 cup freshly grated breadcrumbs

Cook the fusilli and broccoli in a large pan of steadily boiling water until *al dente* with 1 tablespoon of the oil and 1 teaspoon salt.

Meanwhile, heat 4 tablespoons oil in a pan, add the garlic, three anchovy fillets and the chilli pepper. Cook until the garlic is golden-brown, then remove the chilli pepper.

Heat the remaining oil in a clean pan, add the breadcrumbs and the remaining anchovy fillets and cook until golden, stirring constantly.

Drain the pasta and broccoli thoroughly and place in a hot serving dish. Pour the oil and garlic mixture over the top, and sprinkle with the breadcrumb mixture. Season to taste with salt and pepper and serve immediately.

Fusilli alla Contadina

RIGATONI ROSSI
RIGATONI WITH SPICY RED SAUCE

$\frac{1}{4}$ cup butter
2 tablespoons olive oil
2 cloves garlic, finely chopped
1 lb beef tomatoes, skinned, seeded, and chopped
3 red chilli peppers, seeded and finely chopped
1 tablespoon chopped fresh basil
salt, freshly ground black pepper
12 oz rigatoni (ridge-shaped pasta tubes)
$\frac{1}{4}$ cup grated Parmesan cheese

Melt the butter in a pan with 1 tablespoon of the olive oil and cook the chopped garlic until lightly golden. Add the tomatoes, chillis, basil and salt and pepper to taste, then simmer for 10–15 minutes until the sauce thickens.

Meanwhile, cook the rigatoni in a large pan of steadily boiling water until *al dente* with the remaining oil and 1 teaspoon salt. Drain thoroughly, then stir gently into the hot sauce, together with the grated Parmesan cheese. Serve immediately.

RIGATONI CON POMODORI E FUNGHI SECCHI
RIGATONI WITH TOMATO SAUCE AND DRIED MUSHROOMS

$\frac{1}{4}$ cup dried mushrooms
$\frac{1}{4}$ cup butter
2 tablespoons olive oil
1 small onion, finely chopped
1 oz Italian ham, chopped
1 lb plum tomatoes, skinned, seeded and chopped
salt, freshly ground black pepper
$1\frac{1}{2}$ cups rigatoni (ridge-shaped pasta tubes)
$\frac{3}{4}$ cup diced Fontina **or** Bel Paese cheese

Put the dried mushrooms into a bowl and add sufficient water just to cover them; leave for 15 minutes. Drain the mushrooms, straining the soaking liquid and reserving it. Chop the plumped mushrooms.

Melt the butter and 1 tablespoon olive oil in a pan and fry the onion gently until light golden. Add the chopped ham, tomatoes, salt and pepper to taste, the mushrooms and their strained liquid. Simmer the sauce for 10 minutes.

Meanwhile, cook the rigatoni in a large pan of steadily boiling water until *al dente* with the remaining olive oil and 1 teaspoon salt. Drain thoroughly, then stir gently into the prepared hot sauce, together with the cheese. Serve immediately.

Conchiglie alla Carrettiera
PASTA SHELLS WITH OLIVE, HERB AND CAPER SAUCE

1½ cups conchiglie (pasta shells)
8 tablespoons olive oil
salt, freshly ground black pepper
1 large clove of garlic, crushed
1 teaspoon ground ginger
3 tablespoons capers
2 oz ripe olives, pitted and sliced
2 oz green olives, pitted and sliced
1 tablespoon chopped parsley
1 tablespoon chopped fresh thyme
1 tablespoon raisins
1 tablespoon chopped pine nuts

Cook the conchiglie in a large pan of steadily boiling water until *al dente* with 1 tablespoon olive oil and 1 teaspoon salt. Drain thoroughly. Put the remaining olive oil into a clean pan. Add the cooked pasta and stir in the olive oil. Add the remaining ingredients, season to taste and stir all together over gentle heat for 2 minutes until heated through. Serve immediately.

Tagliatelle alla Romana
TAGLIATELLE WITH PECORINO AND PEAS

12 oz fresh peas, shelled
salt, freshly ground black pepper
1½ cups tagliatelle verde
1 tablespoon olive oil
⅓ cup butter, melted
⅓ cup grated Pecorino cheese
¾ cup heavy cream
4 oz Italian ham, cut into thin strips

Cook the peas in a pan of boiling salted water until just tender.

Meanwhile, cook the tagliatelle in a large pan of steadily boiling water until *al dente* with the oil and 1 teaspoon salt.

Drain the peas and the cooked tagliatelle thoroughly and gently stir into the butter over gentle heat. Stir in the Pecorino cheese, cream, strips of ham and salt and pepper to taste. Stir over gentle heat for 1 minute and serve immediately.

PASTA SALADS

A pasta salad can be simple or elaborate, served as an appetizer, an accompaniment to a main course or even as a main course itself. The important thing to remember in each case is that it should have both shape and texture. Undercook the pasta slightly (by 1 minute) so that it keeps its natural shape. Drain it very well, then toss in a prepared dressing while it is still warm; the pasta then has a chance to absorb all the flavors, and the dressing prevents the pasta from sticking together.

SHELL BEAN AND PASTA SALAD

½ cup lumache (pasta snails)
¾ cup olive oil
salt, freshly ground black pepper
1 large clove of garlic, crushed
2 tablespoons chopped fresh sage
1½ lb young shell beans, shelled
3 oz Pecorino cheese, crumbled

Cook the lumache in a large pan of steadily boiling water until almost *al dente* with 1 tablespoon olive oil and 1 teaspoon salt.

Meanwhile, mix the remaining oil with salt and pepper to taste, the garlic and sage.

Drain the cooked pasta thoroughly, then stir in the dressing while the pasta is still warm. Leave to cool thoroughly, then stir in the shelled shell beans and the crumbled Pecorino cheese.

Serve as an appetizer.

ORANGE AND PASTA SALAD

¾ cup farfalle (pasta bows)
1 tablespoon olive oil
salt, freshly ground black pepper
¾ cup sour cream
4 tablespoons fresh orange juice
1 tablespoon chopped fresh mint
2 large oranges, divided into sections
3 scallions, finely chopped

GARNISH

orange slices
mint sprig

Cook the pasta in a large pan of steadily boiling water until almost *al dente* with the olive oil and 1 teaspoon salt.

Meanwhile, mix the sour cream with salt and pepper to taste, the orange juice and the fresh mint.

Drain the cooked pasta thoroughly, then stir in the prepared dressing while the pasta is still warm. Leave to cool slightly, then stir in the orange sections and chopped scallions. Garnish with the orange slices and sprig of mint. Do not chill but serve almost immediately.

Serve as a side salad.

Orange and Pasta Salad

ORIENTAL SALAD

4 large scallions
½ cup conchiglie (pasta shells)
7 tablespoons olive oil
salt, freshly ground black pepper
juice of 1 orange
a pinch of ground ginger
3 teaspoons soy sauce
1 large carrot, coarsely grated
4 oz fresh bean shoots
¼ cucumber, quartered, seeded and diced
2 rings pineapple, fresh **or** canned, and chopped

Trim the scallions to within 2 inches of their base. Cut each bulb piece of onion, at regular intervals lengthways, to within ½ inch of the base. Plunge the prepared onion bulbs into a bowl of iced water so that they open out into 'flowers'. Chop and reserve the top green ends of the scallions.

Cook the conchiglie in a large pan of steadily boiling water until almost *al dente* with 1 tablespoon of the olive oil and 1 teaspoon salt.

Meanwhile, mix the remaining oil with the orange juice, ginger, soy sauce and salt and pepper to taste.

Drain the cooked pasta thoroughly, then stir in the prepared dressing while the pasta is still warm. Leave to cool, then add the carrot, bean shoots, cucumber, chopped pineapple and reserved chopped scallion. Arrange the salad on a flat serving dish and garnish with the scallion 'flowers'.

Serve as a side salad or as a main course.

PASTA WITH AVOCADO AND LEMON SAUCE

1½ cups conchiglie (pasta shells)
3 tablespoons olive oil
salt, freshly ground black pepper
1 large ripe avocado, halved and pitted
grated rind and juice of 1 lemon
1 clove of garlic, crushed
2 teaspoons sugar
3–4 tablespoons milk
4 scallions, chopped
2 tablespoons chopped parsley

Cook the pasta in a large pan of steadily boiling water until almost *al dente* with 1 tablespoon oil and 1 teaspoon salt. Drain thoroughly and toss lightly in the remaining oil while still warm.

Meanwhile, scoop out the avocado flesh and blend until smooth with the lemon rind and juice, the salt and pepper, garlic, sugar and milk. Alternatively, mash the avocado and mix thoroughly with the other ingredients. Stir in the scallions and parsley, thinning the sauce, if liked, with extra milk. Stir the avocado and lemon sauce into the pasta.

Serve as an appetizer or as a side salad.

GINGERED PASTA SALAD

1 cup stelline (star-shaped pasta)
4 tablespoons olive oil
salt, freshly ground black pepper
juice of 1 lemon
2 teaspoons finely shredded fresh ginger
3 oz dried apricots, finely chopped
2 oz golden raisins
4 scallions, chopped
1 tablespoon chopped parsley

GARNISH

1 large orange, divided into sections

Cook the stelline in a large pan of steadily boiling water until almost *al dente* with 1 tablespoon olive oil and 1 teaspoon salt.

Mix the remaining oil with salt and pepper to taste, the lemon juice and the shredded ginger.

Drain the cooked pasta thoroughly, then stir in the dressing while the pasta is still warm, together with the chopped apricots and golden raisins. Leave to cool, then stir in the scallions and chopped parsley. Garnish with the orange sections.

Serve as an appetizer or as a side salad.

GARDEN PASTA SALAD

¾ cup penne (pasta tubes)
7 tablespoons olive oil
salt, freshly ground black pepper
juice of 1 lemon
1 tablespoon chopped parsley
1 tablespoon chopped fresh basil
1 tablespoon chopped watercress
1 tablespoon tomato paste
a generous pinch of sugar
2 carrots, very thinly sliced
2 zucchini, very thinly sliced
1 small onion, cut into thin rings
1 medium leek, cut into matchstick strips
4 radishes, thinly sliced

Cook the pasta shapes in a large pan of steadily boiling water until almost *al dente* with 1 tablespoon olive oil and 1 teaspoon salt.

Meanwhile, mix the lemon juice with the remaining olive oil, the parsley, basil, watercress, tomato paste and sugar. Add seasoning to taste.

Drain the cooked pasta thoroughly, then stir in the prepared dressing while the pasta is still warm. Leave to cool thoroughly, then stir in the sliced carrots, zucchini, onion rings, leek strips and sliced radishes.

Serve as an appetizer or as a side salad.

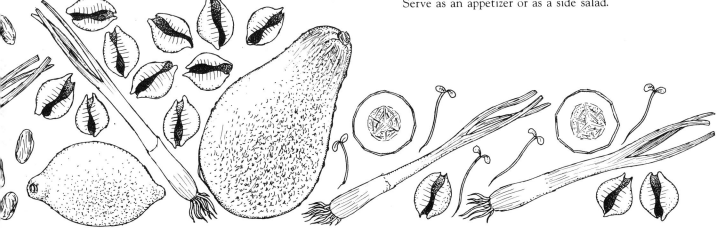

PESTO PASTA SALAD

1½ cups rigatoni (ridge-shaped pasta tubes)
1 tablespoon olive oil
salt, freshly ground black pepper
4 tablespoons Pesto (page 65)
5 stalks celery, chopped
1 sweet red pepper, seeded and diced
1 bunch of scallions, chopped
12 oz canned sweetcorn kernels, drained

GARNISH

4 oz mushrooms, sliced

Cook the rigatoni in a large pan of steadily boiling water until almost *al dente* with the oil and 1 teaspoon salt. Drain thoroughly, then gently stir in the Pesto while the pasta is still warm. Leave to cool, then add the celery, red pepper, scallions and sweetcorn, and mix together well. Arrange the salad on a plate and garnish with the mushrooms.

Serve as a side salad.

PASTA, BEAN AND TUNA SALAD

1 cup maccheroni rigati (ridged macaroni)
7 tablespoons olive oil
salt, freshly ground black pepper
2 tablespoons white wine vinegar
1 tablespoon chopped chives
1 clove of garlic, crushed
finely grated rind of ½ lemon
5 tablespoons canned red kidney beans
7 oz canned tuna, drained and coarsely flaked
4 anchovy fillets, drained and
split lengthways (optional)

Cook the pasta in a large pan of steadily boiling water until almost *al dente* with 1 tablespoon olive oil and 1 teaspoon salt.

Meanwhile, mix the remaining olive oil with the vinegar, chives, garlic, lemon rind and salt and pepper to taste.

Drain the cooked pasta thoroughly, then stir in the prepared dressing while the pasta is still warm. Leave to cool, then stir in the kidney beans and the tuna. Arrange the anchovy fillets on top, if used.

Serve as an appetizer or as a main course.

Pasta, Bean and Tuna Salad

Pasta and Tuna Salad

¾ cup elbow maccheroni
1 tablespoon olive oil
salt, freshly ground black pepper

SAUCE

7 oz canned tuna
6 anchovy fillets, drained
¾ cup Maionese (page 65)
juice of 1 lemon
1 tablespoon capers
1 clove of garlic, crushed
2 tablespoons chopped parsley
white wine, Brodo di Pollo (chicken broth, page 19)
or milk (see Method)

GARNISH

extra capers
extra anchovy fillets, drained
small lemon wedges

Cook the pasta in a large pan of steadily boiling water until almost *al dente* with the oil and 1 teaspoon salt.

Meanwhile, put the tuna into a liquidizer with the anchovy fillets, Maionese, lemon juice, capers, garlic and parsley. Blend until smooth. Alternatively, pound the fish and mix with the other sauce ingredients. If the sauce seems very thick, add a little white wine, chicken broth or milk.

Drain the cooked pasta thoroughly, then stir in the prepared sauce while the pasta is still warm. Chill for 1–2 hours.

Spoon the salad into a serving dish and garnish with extra capers, a criss-cross of anchovy fillets and small lemon wedges. Serve as an appetizer.

Variation
Add a few peeled shrimp to the salad.

Mimosa Pasta Salad

1 cup conchiglie (pasta shells)
5 tablespoons olive oil
salt, freshly ground black pepper
grated rind and juice of 1 lemon
½ cup Maionese (page 65)
8 oz cooked smoked haddock, flaked
3 tablespoons capers
2 hard-cooked eggs
2 tablespoons chopped parsley

Cook the conchiglie in a large pan of steadily boiling water until almost *al dente* with 1 tablespoon olive oil and 1 teaspoon salt.

Meanwhile, mix together the remaining olive oil with the lemon rind and juice and salt and pepper to taste.

Drain the pasta thoroughly, then stir in the prepared dressing while the pasta is still warm. Leave to cool, then mix in the Maionese, flaked haddock and capers. Separate the whites and yolks from the hard-cooked eggs. Chop the whites finely, and sieve the yolks. Stir the chopped egg white into the pasta mixture and spoon into a serving dish. Sprinkle with the chopped parsley and then with the sieved hard-cooked egg yolk.

Serve as a side salad or as a main course.

Sweet Sour Pasta and Chicken Salad

1 medium eggplant, cut into ½ inch cubes
salt, freshly ground black pepper
¾ cup wholewheat pasta rings
¾ cup olive oil
3 tablespoons white wine vinegar
6 tablespoons tomato juice
a squeeze of lemon juice
1 tablespoon sugar
1 clove of garlic, chopped
8 oz cooked chicken, chopped

Put the eggplant cubes into a colander and sprinkle generously with salt, then leave to drain for 30 minutes.

Meanwhile, cook the pasta rings in a large pan of steadily boiling water until almost *al dente* with 1 tablespoon of the oil and 1 teaspoon salt.

Mix the vinegar with the tomato juice, 4 tablespoons olive oil, the lemon juice, sugar, garlic and salt and pepper to taste.

Pat the eggplant dry on absorbent paper. Put the remaining oil in a pan and fry the eggplant gently until lightly golden. (If the eggplant is very porous, it may require a little extra oil.)

Drain the pasta thoroughly, then stir in the prepared dressing together with the fried eggplant cubes and the chopped chicken. Chill thoroughly before serving.

Serve as an appetizer or as a main course.

Chicken and Artichoke Salad

¾ cup farfalle (pasta bows)
7 tablespoons olive oil
salt, freshly ground black pepper
2 tablespoons white wine vinegar
2 tablespoons chopped parsley
1 clove of garlic, crushed
1 teaspoon French mustard
6 oz smoked chicken, divided into strips (see **Note**)
6 canned artichoke hearts, quartered
3 tablespoons sour cream

GARNISH

paprika

Cook the farfalle in a large pan of steadily boiling water until almost *al dente* with 1 tablespoon of the oil and 1 teaspoon salt.

Meanwhile, mix the remaining olive oil with the vinegar, salt and pepper to taste, the parsley, garlic and mustard.

Drain the cooked farfalle thoroughly, then stir in the prepared dressing while the pasta is still warm. Leave to cool, then mix in the strips of chicken and quartered artichoke hearts. Spoon the salad into a serving dish and top with the sour cream. Sprinkle with paprika.

Serve as a side salad or as a main course.

Note Smoked chicken is obtainable from good delicatessens. Use plainly cooked chicken if smoked chicken is not available.

Italian Ham and Pasta Salad

Serves 6

1 cup anelli (pasta rings)
1 tablespoon olive oil
salt, freshly ground black pepper
$\frac{3}{4}$ cup sour cream
1 tablespoon lemon juice
1 tablespoon chopped chives
8 oz Italian ham, chopped
2 oranges, divided into sections
4 oz cooked shell beans

GARNISH

grated orange rind

Cook the pasta in a large pan of steadily boiling water until almost *al dente* with the oil and 1 teaspoon salt.

Meanwhile, mix together the sour cream, lemon juice and chopped chives, and season to taste.

Drain the pasta thoroughly and toss in the dressing while still warm. Leave to cool, then add the ham, orange sections and beans, and adjust seasoning to taste. Garnish with the orange rind.

Serve as an appetizer or as a main course.

Smoked Salmon and Avocado Pasta Salad

1 cup conchiglie (pasta shells)
7 tablespoons olive oil
salt, freshly ground black pepper
3 tablespoons lemon juice
$\frac{1}{2}$ teaspoon French mustard
4 oz smoked salmon, sliced into thin strips
6 oz shelled shrimp
1 large avocado, peeled, pitted and scooped into balls
6 scallions, finely chopped
1 tablespoon chopped parsley

GARNISH

unpeeled shrimp
lettuce leaves

Cook the pasta in a large pan of steadily boiling water until almost *al dente* with 1 tablespoon oil and 1 teaspoon salt.

Meanwhile, mix together the lemon juice, remaining oil, the mustard and salt and pepper to taste.

Drain the pasta thoroughly and stir in the prepared dressing. Leave to cool, then add the salmon, shrimp, avocado, scallions and chopped parsley. Garnish with unshelled shrimp and serve on a bed of lettuce.

Serve as an appetizer.

Smoked Salmon and Avocado Pasta Salad

PASTA SAUCES

This is one of the most important chapters in the book, as a sauce that is served with pasta can either make or mar the finished dish.

The sauces of Italy, particularly those that are often served with pasta, differ greatly from the sauces of most other countries. With some exceptions, few are thickened with flour, and many savory ones are based on olive oil. Cream is added to savory sauces less frequently than it is to sweet sauces.

The best known sauce has to be *Bolognese*, sometimes referred to as *Ragu* (see page 29 – Spaghetti Bolognese). This classic meat sauce is traditionally served with spaghetti, but can accompany almost any cooked pasta.

Some sauces can be frozen. It is important, however, to thaw them completely before use. Re-heat in a double boiler or in a bowl over a pan of hot water. As many separate upon being chilled or thawed, they should be stirred before being re-heated.

SALSA BESCIAMELLA
SAVOURY WHITE SAUCE

Makes 3 cups (approx)

3½ cups milk
2 bay leaves
1 small onion, peeled and stuck with 2 cloves
a small sprig of fresh thyme
3 tablespoons butter
6 tablespoons flour
salt, freshly ground black pepper
a generous pinch of ground mace

Put the milk into a pan with the bay leaves, onion and cloves and the thyme. Bring to the boil slowly, then cover the pan and leave to stand, off the heat, for about 45 minutes.

Melt the butter in a clean pan. Stir in the flour and cook gently for 1 minute, stirring all the time. Add the strained flavored milk slowly, beating well between each addition. Once all the milk has been incorporated, bring the sauce to the boil. Reduce the heat and simmer gently for 10–15 minutes until the sauce has thickened and reduced slightly. Season to taste with salt, pepper and mace.

Use for baked pasta dishes.

Note   This sauce can be made 24 hours in advance and kept chilled. It can be frozen for up to 6 months.

Variation
For a thicker sauce, either add a little extra flour to the melted butter, or simmer the sauce for longer. (The longer the sauce is cooked, the greater will be the depth of flavor. Take care, however, that it does not burn.)

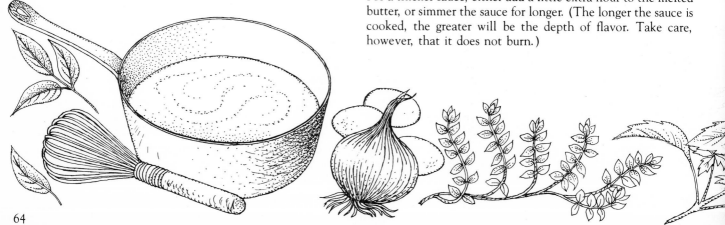

MAIONESE
ITALIAN MAYONNAISE

Makes 2 cups (approx)

3 egg yolks
1 tablespoon white wine vinegar
1½ cups olive oil
1 clove of garlic, crushed
salt, freshly ground black pepper
2 tablespoons chopped fresh basil
1–2 tablespoons hot water (see Method)

Beat the egg yolks in a bowl to break them up. Beat in the white wine vinegar, and then gradually add the olive oil in a fine trickle, beating all the time, until all the olive oil has been incorporated. Add the garlic, salt and pepper to taste and the fresh basil. If the mayonnaise is too thick, thin to the desired consistency with a little hot water.

Use for pasta salads.

Note Maionese can be chilled for up to 24 hours in a covered container. It should not be frozen.

PESTO
HERB AND PINE NUT SAUCE

Makes 1½ cups (approx)

a good sized bunch of fresh basil leaves
4 garlic cloves, peeled
3 tablespoons pine nuts
salt, freshly ground black pepper
1 cup olive oil

Trim off the excess stalks from the basil leaves. Put the leaves into a liquidizer or food processor with the garlic, pine nuts, salt and pepper to taste and half the olive oil. Blend until smooth and then gradually add the remaining olive oil.

Use for plainly cooked pasta. Stir into cooked tagliatelle or fettucine.

Note Pesto is traditionally made with a pestle and mortar. The basil, garlic, pine kernels and seasoning are ground until they form a paste. The oil is then gradually added, a little at a time, until the sauce is smooth.

Pesto can be stored in a covered container in a refrigerator for up to 1 week. It is not suitable for freezing.

Variation
If preparing Pesto manually, substitute ground almonds for the pine nuts. Finely chop the basil, crush the garlic and mix the ingredients together.

SALSA DI DRAGONCELLO
TARRAGON SAUCE

Makes 1½ cups (approx)

2 tablespoons chopped fresh tarragon
7 tablespoons Brodo di Pollo
(chicken broth, page 19)
7 tablespoons dry white wine
salt, freshly ground black pepper
6 tablespoons spinach purée
(frozen chopped spinach can be used)
⅓ cup butter
freshly grated nutmeg

Put the chopped tarragon, chicken broth, wine and salt and pepper to taste into a pan. Bring to the boil and boil steadily until the liquor has almost evaporated. Add the spinach purée and heat through.

Melt the butter in a pan until it turns golden; do not allow it to burn. Beat the butter into the tarragon and spinach purée, and season with the nutmeg. Heat through but do not allow the sauce to boil.

Use for cooked short cut and shaped pastas.

Note This sauce should be used fresh. It is not suitable for storage.

SALSA DI FEGATINI
CHICKEN LIVER SAUCE

Makes 2 cups sauce

3 tablespoons butter
1 small onion, finely chopped
8 oz chicken livers, chopped finely
4 tablespoons flour
4 oz mushrooms, finely chopped
7 tablespoons Brodo di Manzo (beef broth, page 20)
7 tablespoons red wine
4 tablespoons Marsala
juice of 1 orange
salt, freshly ground black pepper

Melt the butter in a pan and gently fry the chopped onion for 4–5 minutes. Add the chicken livers and fry gently until sealed on all sides. Sprinkle the flour over the chicken livers, stirring it in. Add the mushrooms and gradually stir in the beef broth, wine, Marsala and orange juice. Simmer until the livers are tender and the sauce very thick. Season to taste with salt and pepper.

Serve as a topping sauce for plainly cooked pasta.

Note This sauce can be chilled for 24 hours and frozen for 1 month.

Salsa Genovese
GENOESE VEAL SAUCE

Makes 2 cups (approx)

3 tablespoons butter
1 medium onion, thinly sliced
3 stalks celery, finely chopped
1 large carrot, finely chopped
8 oz lean veal, finely chopped **or** ground
1 clove of garlic, crushed
1 tablespoon flour
¾ cup red wine
¾ cup Brodo di Manzo (beef broth, page 20)
salt, freshly ground black pepper
2 tablespoons Pesto (page 65)

Melt the butter in a pan and gently fry the onion for 4–5 minutes. Add the celery, carrot and veal, and fry until the meat is evenly browned. Stir in the garlic and the flour. Gradually add the wine and broth, and bring to the boil. Season to taste with salt and pepper and add the Pesto. Reduce the heat and simmer the sauce for 20–25 minutes.

Use for plainly cooked long pasta.

Note This sauce can be chilled for 24 hours. It can be frozen for 1 month.

Variation
Soak 1 tablespoon chopped or sliced dried mushrooms in warm water for 15 minutes. Drain well and add to the sauce when frying the celery, carrot and veal.

Salsa di Gamberi
SHRIMP SAUCE

Makes 1½ cups (approx)

8 oz unshelled shrimp
a sprig of fresh fennel **or** ½ teaspoon dried fennel
¾ cup dry white wine
a strip of lemon rind
¾ cup Italian dry vermouth
salt, freshly ground black pepper
2 tablespoons butter
1 small onion, finely chopped
1 tablespoon flour
4 tablespoons heavy cream
2 tablespoons chopped parsley

Shell the shrimp and put to one side. Put the shells into a pan with the fennel, white wine, lemon rind, vermouth and salt and pepper to taste. Simmer until the liquor has reduced by one-third, then strain it.

Melt the butter in a pan and gently fry the onion for 3–4 minutes. Stir in the flour and cook for 1 minute. Gradually add the shrimp liquor, stirring constantly. Bring to the boil, then reduce the heat and simmer the sauce for 2–3 minutes. Stir in the cream, the reserved shrimp and chopped parsley and heat through.

Use for cooked pasta shapes.

Note This sauce should be used fresh. It is not suitable for storage.

SALSA ALLA VENETA
VENETIAN LOBSTER SAUCE

Makes 1 cup (approx)

6 tablespoons olive oil
3 cloves garlic, finely chopped
4 oz chopped cooked lobster meat
6 anchovy fillets, drained and chopped
2 tablespoons chopped parsley
1 tablespoon red wine vinegar
salt, freshly ground black pepper

Heat the oil in a pan and gently fry the chopped garlic for 1 minute. Add the remaining ingredients and boil quite quickly for 1–2 minutes until reduced.

Use for cooked pasta shells.

Note   This sauce should be used immediately. It is not suitable for storage.

SALSA DI VONGOLE
CLAM SAUCE

Makes 3½ cups (approx)

1 tablespoon olive oil
1 onion, finely chopped
9 oz canned clams, drained
1 lb plum tomatoes, skinned, seeded and chopped
1 teaspoon fresh mixed herbs
¾ cup white wine
salt, freshly ground black pepper

Heat the oil in a pan and cook the onion until soft. Add the clams, chopped tomatoes, herbs and wine, and season to taste with salt and pepper. Simmer the sauce for 5 minutes.

Use for cooked long pasta.

Note   This sauce should be used fresh. It is not suitable for storage.

SALSA AGRODOLCE
ITALIAN SWEET AND SOUR SAUCE

Makes 1½ cups (approx)

3 tablespoons butter
1 large onion, finely chopped
2 tablespoons flour
¾ cup Brodo di Manzo (beef broth, page 20)
¾ cup red wine
3 tablespoons Marsala
3 tablespoons white wine vinegar
finely grated rind of ½ orange
2 tablespoons golden raisins
1 tablespoon pine nuts, chopped
2 tablespoons sugar
3 tablespoons water
2 tablespoons bitter chocolate, grated
salt, freshly ground black pepper

Melt the butter in a pan and gently fry the onion for 4 minutes. Stir in the flour and cook for 1 minute. Gradually stir in the beef broth and wine, and bring to the boil. Add the Marsala, white wine vinegar, orange rind, golden raisins and pine nuts, reduce the heat and simmer for 15 minutes.

Meanwhile, put the sugar and water into a small pan and stir over gentle heat until the sugar has dissolved. Boil steadily until the syrup turns caramel in color. Stir the caramel into the sauce, together with the grated chocolate and salt and pepper to taste. Heat the sauce through until the chocolate has melted and the sauce is glossy.

Use for plainly cooked shaped pasta. Alternatively, spoon the sauce over cooked noodles when serving them as an accompaniment to cooked poultry or game.

Note   This sauce should be used fresh. It is not suitable for storage.

AGLIATA
GARLIC AND BREADCRUMB SAUCE

Makes 1 cup (approx)

3 garlic cloves, crushed
4 tablespoons fresh white breadcumbs
1 tablespoon white wine vinegar
salt, freshly ground black pepper
$\frac{3}{4}$ cup olive oil

Put the crushed garlic, breadcrumbs, vinegar and salt and pepper to taste into a bowl. Mix in the olive oil until the sauce is smooth.

Use for plainly cooked pasta. Stir into cooked tagliatelle or fettucine.

Note Agliata can be chilled for 3–4 days. It is not suitable for freezing.

SALSA VERDE AL RAFANO
GREEN HORSERADISH SAUCE

Makes 1½ cups (approx)

12 oz plum tomatoes, skinned, seeded and chopped
1 clove of garlic, crushed
3 tablespoons fine fresh breadcrumbs
2 tablespoons chopped parsley
1 tablespoon finely chopped mint
1 tablespoon freshly grated horseradish
$\frac{3}{4}$ cup olive oil (approx)
salt, freshly ground black pepper

Mix the chopped tomatoes with the garlic, breadcrumbs, parsley, mint and horseradish. Beat in the oil until it is evenly absorbed. Add more oil if a thinner sauce is required. Season to taste with salt and pepper.

Use for pasta salads.

Note This sauce should be used fresh. It is not suitable for storage.

SALSA DI GORGONZOLA
CREAMY GORGONZOLA SAUCE

Makes 2 cups (approx)

1½ cups heavy cream
2 tablespoons Marsala
6 oz Gorgonzola, finely crumbled
1 clove of garlic, crushed
salt, freshly ground black pepper

Put the cream into a pan with the Marsala, and heat through. Add the Gorgonzola and stir over gentle heat until the cheese has dissolved and the sauce is creamy. Stir in the garlic and add salt and pepper to taste.

Use for plainly cooked long pasta.

Note This sauce can be chilled for 24 hours. It is not suitable for freezing.

SALSA DI NOCI
WALNUT AND PARSLEY SAUCE

Makes 1½ cups (approx)

3 oz ground walnuts
$\frac{1}{4}$ cup butter, melted
3 tablespoons fine fresh breadcrumbs
4 tablespoons finely chopped parsley
$\frac{3}{4}$ cup olive oil
salt, freshly ground black pepper
3 tablespoons heavy cream
a pinch of grated nutmeg

Mix the ground walnuts with the melted butter and the breadcrumbs. Stir in the parsley and gradually beat in the oil. Add salt and pepper to taste, the cream and nutmeg. Blend in a liquidizer or food processor if a very smooth sauce is required.

Serve cold with plainly cooked hot pasta – home-made tagliatelle or fettucine are perfect choices.

Note This sauce should be used fresh. It is not suitable for storage.

BAGNA CAUDA
GARLIC AND OLIVE OIL SAUCE

Makes 1½ cups (approx)

¾ cup olive oil
½ cup butter
8 anchovy fillets, drained and finely chopped
2–3 cloves garlic, crushed
freshly ground black pepper

Put the oil and butter into a small casserole or fondue pot. Stand over the heat and stir until the butter and oil are evenly melted and hot. Add the anchovy fillets, garlic and pepper to taste (salt is not necessary), and stir.

Serve piping hot with cooked pasta shapes.

Note This sauce is traditionally served in the Piedmont region of Italy in the same way as a fondue; the sauce is put into a small flameproof pan over a table burner, and surrounded by a selection of raw vegetables to use as dippers. It is equally delicious however, if cooked pasta shapes are served as accompanying dippers. It should be used fresh.

SALSA ROSSA
RED SAUCE

Makes 1½ cups (approx)

3 tablespoons olive oil
1 large onion, thinly sliced
2 medium green peppers, seeded and thinly sliced
1 lb plum tomatoes, skinned, seeded and chopped
¼ teaspoon chilli powder
salt
Brodo di Manzo (beef broth, page 20) **or**
red wine (see Method)

Heat the oil in a pan and gently fry the onion for 3–4 minutes. Add the peppers and tomatoes, and cook gently until the vegetables become soft and squashy. Add the chilli powder and salt to taste, and simmer the sauce for 5–10 minutes. This sauce is naturally very thick but it can be thinned by the addition of broth or red wine.

Use for cooked long or shaped pastas.

Note This sauce can be chilled for 24 hours. It can be frozen for 6 months.

Bagna Cauda

SUGO DI POMODORO E PANNA
TOMATO AND CREAM SAUCE

Makes 1 quart (approx)

½ cup butter
1 medium onion, finely chopped
1 medium carrot, finely chopped
2 stalks celery, finely chopped
1½ lb ripe plum tomatoes,
skinned, seeded and roughly chopped
¾ cup Brodo di Pollo (chicken broth, page 19) **or**
dry white wine
1 clove of garlic, crushed
salt, freshly ground black pepper
a pinch of sugar
1 tablespoon chopped fresh basil
2 tablespoons tomato paste
¾ cup heavy cream

Melt the butter in a pan and gently fry the onion, carrot and celery for 5 minutes until soft. Stir in the other ingredients apart from the cream, and bring to the boil. Reduce the heat and simmer gently for 20 minutes.

Blend the sauce in a liquidizer or food processor, or sieve it until smooth. Return to a clean pan and stir in the cream. Heat through gently and adjust seasoning to taste.

Serve as a topping sauce or use for baked pasta dishes.

Note This sauce can be chilled for 2 hours. It can be frozen for 6 months.

SALSA DI POMODORO
FRESH TOMATO SAUCE

Makes 2 cups (approx)

2¼ lb plum tomatoes, roughly chopped
1 medium onion, finely chopped
1 large carrot, chopped
3 stalks celery, finely chopped
2 cloves garlic, crushed
1 tablespoon chopped fresh thyme
1 tablespoon chopped fresh basil
1 teaspoon sugar
2 tablespoons tomato paste
salt, freshly ground black pepper
Brodo di Pollo (chicken broth, page 19)

Put all the ingredients into a large pan. Cover, and bring to the boil, then reduce the heat and simmer gently for about 30 minutes until the tomatoes are pulpy and all the other vegetables quite soft.

Sieve the sauce, then re-heat to serve, adjusting the consistency by adding a little chicken broth, if liked.

Serve as a topping sauce or use for baked pasta dishes.

Note This sauce can be chilled for 24 hours. It can be frozen for 6 months.

Variation
Add 1–2 teaspoons anchovy extract and 8 anchovy fillets, drained and finely chopped to the above.

SALSA DI ARANCI
WHISKED ORANGE SAUCE

Makes 1½ cups (approx)

6 egg yolks
2 tablespoons orange flower water
2 oz sugar
3 tablespoons heavy cream

Whisk the egg yolks with the orange flower water and sugar until light and creamy. Put into the top of a double boiler, or in a bowl over a pan of hot water. Add the cream, then stir the sauce over gentle heat until it is thick enough to coat the back of a wooden spoon. Remove the pan from the heat and serve the sauce immediately poured over the top of freshly cooked pasta.

Note Serve fresh. This sauce is not suitable for storage.

SALSA DI CIOCCOLATO
ITALIAN CHOCOLATE SAUCE

Makes 2 cups (approx)

1½ cups light cream
3 oz semisweet chocolate
2 tablespoons Amaretto liqueur
2 tablespoons butter
1 tablespoon flour
1 tablespoon vanilla sugar
2 egg yolks

Put the cream and chocolate into a saucepan and stir over very gentle heat until the chocolate has melted. Remove from the heat, stir in the Amaretto and leave to cool.
  Melt the butter in a pan, then stir in the flour and cook gently for 1 minute. Gradually stir in the cream and melted chocolate. Bring to the boil and stir until the sauce has thickened. Stir in the sugar, beat in the egg yolks, and heat the sauce through without allowing it to boil. Use for plainly cooked pasta.

Note Serve fresh. This sauce is not suitable for storage.

SALSA DI PESCHE E AMARETTI
PEACH AND MACAROON SAUCE

Makes 2 cups (approx)

3 large, ripe peaches
¼ cup sugar
8 Amaretti (small macaroons), finely crushed
finely grated rind of ½ orange
1 cup light cream

Nick the skin at the stalk end of each peach. Plunge into a bowl of boiling water for 45 seconds, then remove the peaches and slide off the skins. Cut each peach around the middle; twist to separate the two halves, then remove the stones. Sieve the peach flesh, then mix the purée with the sugar, crushed Amaretti, orange rind and cream. Use for cooked long or shaped pasta.

Note Serve fresh. This sauce is not suitable for storage.

SALSA DI STREGA
STREGA SAUCE

Makes 8 oz (approx)

½ cup unsalted butter
1 cup soft brown sugar
3 tablespoons Strega liqueur
2 tablespoons ground almonds
finely grated rind of ½ lemon
a generous pinch of ground cinnamon

Beat the butter until it is soft and light, then beat in the sugar and Strega until soft and smooth. Add the ground almonds, lemon rind and cinnamon, and mix together well.
  Serve on top of freshly cooked pasta, or as below.

Note This is really a sweet 'butter'. Make it up in advance, cover with wax paper and roll up. Store in a refrigerator or freezer for 2–3 days. It is then ready for melting and tossing with cooked noodles or pasta shapes for a quick dessert.

Sweet Pasta Recipes

Pasta is just as versatile when used in a sweet context as it is in a savory one; indeed, it was particularly popular in the eighteenth and nineteenth centuries when it was often eaten with sticky sweet sauces. Remember to precede pasta desserts with a light main course.

A simple way of presenting a sweet pasta dish is to cook the pasta in exactly the same way as for savory recipes, then to top or mix it with a sweet sauce, cream or nuts. Alternatively, it can merely be tossed in melted butter with the addition of sugar and spices.

Tagliatelle with Kiwi Fruit

1 cup tagliatelle
1 tablespoon olive oil
1 teaspoon salt
3 tablespoons butter
rind and juice of 1 large orange
2 tablespoons sugar
1 tablespoon brandy

DECORATION

2 kiwi fruit, peeled and sliced
1 tablespoon flaked almonds, lightly toasted

Cook the tagliatelle in a large pan of steadily boiling water until *al dente* with the olive oil and salt.

Meanwhile, melt the butter in a pan over gentle heat, then add the orange rind and juice and the sugar, and stir until the sugar has dissolved. Stir in the brandy and heat through.

Drain the cooked tagliatelle thoroughly and toss quickly with the hot orange butter. Transfer to a serving dish and decorate with the sliced kiwi fruit and the flaked almonds.

Serve with whipped cream.

Tagliatelle with Kiwi Fruit

TAGLIATELLE WITH STRAWBERRY SAUCE

12 oz strawberries, hulled and halved
2 oz vanilla sugar **or** powdered sugar
juice of 1 lemon
3 tablespoons Cointreau
1 cup tagliatelle
1 tablespoon olive oil
1 teaspoon salt
$\frac{3}{4}$ cup light cream

DECORATION

2 tablespoons flaked almonds, lightly toasted

Put the strawberries into a shallow dish and sprinkle with the sugar, lemon juice and Cointreau. Cover and chill for 2–3 hours.

Meanwhile, cook the tagliatelle in a large pan of steadily boiling water until *al dente* with the oil and salt. Drain thoroughly and toss over gentle heat with the light cream. Transfer the pasta to a serving dish and top with the chilled strawberries and their juices. Sprinkle with the toasted almonds and serve immediately.

SEVILLE SHELL SURPRISE

1 cup conchiglie (pasta shells)
1 tablespoon olive oil
1 teaspoon salt
juice of 2 oranges
finely grated rind of 1 orange
$\frac{1}{4}$ cup butter
$\frac{1}{2}$ cup sugar
4 tablespoons heavy cream
1 large orange, divided into sections

DECORATION

2 tablespoons chopped hazelnuts

Cook the pasta shells in a large pan of steadily boiling water until *al dente* with the olive oil and salt.

Meanwhile, put the orange juice into a pan with the orange rind, butter, sugar and heavy cream. Stir over gentle heat until the sugar has dissolved and the mixture is well blended. Add the orange sections.

Drain the cooked pasta shells thoroughly and stir into the hot orange sauce. Transfer to a serving dish and sprinkle with the hazelnuts. Serve immediately with ice cream.

Note This recipe is particularly delicious when accompanied by chocolate ice cream.

JUBILEE PASTA

1 cup lumache (pasta snails)
1 tablespoon olive oil
1 teaspoon salt
14 oz canned bing cherries, pitted
2 tablespoons bing cherry jam
juice of 1 orange
2 teaspoons cornstarch
2 tablespoons brandy

Cook the lumache in a large pan of steadily boiling water until *al dente* with the olive oil and salt.

Meanwhile, drain the cherries and put their juice into a pan. Add the jam to the cherry juice and stir over gentle heat until the jam has dissolved. Blend the orange juice and cornstarch to a smooth paste, and stir in a little of the hot cherry liquor. Return to the remaining juice in the pan, and stir over gentle heat until the cherry juice thickens. Stir in the brandy.

Drain the cooked pasta thoroughly and transfer to a serving dish. Spoon the hot cherry sauce over the top and serve immediately with whipped cream or ice cream.

PASTA WITH FUDGE SAUCE

1 cup fettucine
1 tablespoon olive oil
1 teaspoon salt
$\frac{1}{3}$ cup butter
$\frac{2}{3}$ cup soft brown sugar
4 oz chopped marshmallows
3 tablespoons heavy cream
a few drops butterscotch extract

Cook the fettucine in a large pan of steadily boiling water until *al dente* with the olive oil and salt.

Meanwhile, put the butter, sugar, marshmallows and cream into a pan, and stir over gentle heat until melted. Add butterscotch extract to taste.

Drain the cooked fettucine thoroughly and transfer to a serving dish. Spoon the hot fudge sauce over the top and serve immediately.

FRESH FIG AND PASTA DESSERT

8 fresh figs, chopped
4 tablespoons Maraschino liqueur
1 cup farfalle (pasta bows)
1 tablespoon olive oil
1 teaspoon salt
6 oz fresh raspberries
2 oz Amaretti (small macaroons), finely crumbled
¾ cup heavy cream, lightly whipped

DECORATION

crumbled Amaretti

Put the figs into a bowl with the Maraschino liqueur; cover and chill for 1 hour.

Meanwhile, cook the farfalle in a large pan of steadily boiling water until *al dente* with the oil and salt.

Sieve the fresh raspberries and mix with the crumbled Amaretti and the heavy cream. Stir in the chilled figs and their juices.

Drain the pasta thoroughly, reserve four bows and transfer the rest to individual serving dishes. Top each dish with the prepared fruit and cream sauce, decorate with the crumbled Amaretti and reserved pasta bows, and serve immediately.

BANANA BOWS

1 cup farfalle (pasta bows)
1 tablespoon olive oil
1 teaspoon salt
8 oz clear honey
grated rind and juice of 2 lemons
4 oz raisins
2 oz candied cherries, chopped
¼ cup butter
2 bananas, cut into diagonal slices

Cook the farfalle in a large pan of steadily boiling water until *al dente* with the oil and salt.

Meanwhile, heat the honey, lemon rind and juice, the raisins and chopped cherries in a pan.

Melt the butter in a clean pan and fry the sliced banana for 2–3 minutes until lightly golden.

Drain the pasta thoroughly, then gently stir in the hot honey sauce and the fried banana. Transfer to a serving dish and serve immediately.

Fresh Fig and Pasta Dessert

INDEX OF RECIPES